D0548399

WITHDRAWN
FROM
STOCK

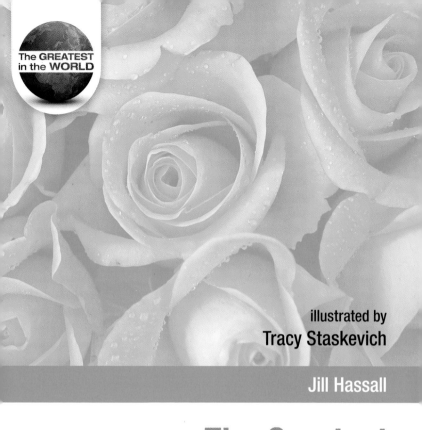

The GREATEST
in the WORLD

illustrated by
Tracy Staskevich

Jill Hassall

The Greatest
Wedding
Tips in the World

A 'The Greatest in the World' book

www.thegreatestintheworld.com

Illustrations:
Tracy Staskevich

Typesetting:
BR Typesetting

Cover images:
© Simone van den Berg; © foto.fritz; © Mat Hayward;
© Eric Limon; © Tan Kian Khoon
all courtesy of www.fotolia.com

Copy editor:
Bronwyn Robertson
www.theartsva.com

Series creator/editor:
Steve Brookes

Published in 2008 by
The Greatest in the World Ltd, PO Box 3182,
Stratford-upon-Avon, Warwickshire CV37 7XW

Text and Illustrations Copyright © 2008 – The Greatest in the World Ltd.

A CIP catalogue record for this book is available from the British Library
ISBN 978-1-905151-27-1

Printed and bound in China by 1010 Printing International Ltd.

To Colin with all my love.

Without you,
none of this would have been possible.

A few words from Jill…

So you've done it! You've found the man of your dreams and have named the day. Note here, that I'm addressing the bride. More on the bridegroom later, but be assured, that unless the man you've managed to get to propose to you is a real 'New Man', the rest of the wedding will fall on your shoulders. He might tag along to wedding fairs and make suitable noises in the background, but the decisions will undoubtedly be all yours. The best you can hope for is that he will turn up, suitably dressed, on the day.

There are two things you've got to be prepared for when planning a wedding. The first is the cost. Forget the amount you first thought of – the final cost will be at least four times that. But hopefully this book will help you save money while still having the wedding of your dreams.

The second thing is that there will be rows and arguments. Big, fiery fights or small smouldering resentments, there has probably never yet been a wedding without them. You might smile and say it couldn't happen to you – but don't believe it. It could be the choice of venue, the bridesmaids, or the guest list but arguments there will be! After 10 years of running a wedding business, I've seen it all!

This book will guide you through the minefield of planning your wedding so that you can walk down the aisle on your big day, confident that everything will go well because everything that could possibly go wrong has been avoided.

Good luck! *Jill*

Contents

Love does not
consist of gazing
at each other but
in looking forward
in the same direction.

Antoine de Saint-Exupéry

So you've named the day

chapter 1

chapter 1
So you've named the day

You're engaged! You've named the day! Now the fun starts. This book aims to take you through all the preparations for your special day so that you can enjoy a wedding without stress. It is based on church and civil ceremonies within the English legal system but members of other faiths will also find it invaluable. In addition, I have included some of the traditions and superstitions connected with weddings.

I haven't given prices and fees as they vary so much throughout the country and change from year to year. However, there are plenty of money-saving ideas so you can keep within your budget.

Quick tip

BE PREPARED!

When planning a wedding the golden rule to remember is that, at some time, you will offend someone. It might be your parents, your future in-laws or parents of hopeful bridesmaids. Don't worry; stay calm and the argument will blow over. Just remember that it is YOUR wedding and while you want to try and keep everyone happy, it's not always possible. You are not alone. It happens to ALL couples!

The law

All weddings in England and Wales must take place in an Anglican church or any other religious building that is registered for the solemnization of marriage, a Register Office, or a building approved for civil marriage.

If you want to get married in a Church of England or Church in Wales, you should speak to the vicar of the parish. Normally, you would not also need to see the Registrar of your district.

For other religious buildings, you first of all need to speak to the person in charge of marriages. You will need to give notice at the Register Office(s) of the district(s) in which you live. Some faiths will require you to also book the services of a Registrar in order to register the marriage. (See how to do this in the Civil Marriage section.)

Second time around

If this is to be a second marriage after divorce for either of the couple and you wish to be married in church, you need to speak to the minister first. Many Church of England churches will not allow divorced people to remarry in church, although they may well offer a blessing ceremony. However, some of the non-conformist churches will allow remarriage after divorce.

You will need to produce evidence that you are free to remarry. This will be either a Decree Absolute in the case of a divorced person or a Death Certificate if the person has been widowed.

WHAT IF . . . ?

What happens if the reception venue is double booked?
What happens if your wedding dress shop goes bankrupt?
No, you don't want to think of things like that happening to
you, but they can. The bigger the wedding, the more things
there are to go wrong so wedding insurance is a MUST.

A specialist wedding insurance package can cost as little
as £60, but when you think that the average wedding these
days runs into thousands, it's a minor expense that can be
worth every penny if things go wrong.

You can get details of wedding insurance packages
from any of the big insurance companies but also check
out leaflets at wedding fairs. Many smaller specialist
companies, and even supermarkets, offer very good deals.

Ideas!

Have an idea of the type of wedding you want before you
start booking anything. If you want the traditional church
white wedding, then you will need to look for suitable venues.
However, you might want to be different and have some sort
of themed wedding, e.g. Mediaeval or Roaring Twenties. In that
case, it is no use booking somewhere totally out of keeping
with the theme.

Changing your mind after booking a venue can be very costly
as you would almost certainly lose your deposit.

Research

In these hi-tech days, it's easy to find all your wedding requirements on the internet and this can save loads of time. However, seeing places or things on a screen can be misleading. Reception rooms, for example, can look huge in photographs, but in reality can be very cramped. Unless you live far from the area you've chosen to get married in, it's important that you view everything in person. That way, you won't be disappointed on the day.

Quick tip

MAKE A LIST

Make a list of all the jobs to be done and tick them off as you go. It's a good idea to make a wedding calendar—you can use a cheap diary—to show when final meetings have to take place and when deposits and final payments have to be made. You don't want to find that your cars have been cancelled because you forgot to pay the balance.

Help or hindrance?

You might want to accept any offers of help going, especially if it eases your financial burden. But sometimes, things can get a bit fraught and, having seen her handiwork, you don't want Aunty Olive to make your bouquet/dress/cake. Time to be tactful. A good way out is to invent a mythical friend and say gently, "I'm so sorry. Mary at work offered and I've already told her I'm using Flowers'r'Us. She'd be so offended if she found out you were doing them, I might even lose my job . . ."

Paying the bills

Many couples find it useful to set up a separate wedding account with their bank. This means they can put in regular amounts of money to be used solely for the wedding, without having to dip into their everyday budget.

Who pays what?

Traditionally the bride's parents footed the bill for the whole day but these days, luckily for them, things are far more flexible. Some couples choose to pay for everything themselves; others share with both sets of parents. If this is going to be the case, it is diplomatic to set up a meeting with the family and discuss who is going to pay for what. It's not a good idea to simply tell one set of parents that they are expected to dig deep!

The guest list

Who to ask? This is always big problem and will be where you'll wish the two of you had just eloped! Your budget will have a big bearing on this—see Reception section for calculations—but once you have your number, it's time to sit down and work out your list. The obvious people are your immediate families, plus your attendants and best man.

It is diplomatic to try to get an even number on both sides, but if the bride's parents are footing the bill, they might feel that they are entitled to invite more guests than the groom. Sometimes, one person has a much bigger family and circle of friends than the other, so this will have to be taken into consideration as well.

> **Love is composed of a single soul inhabiting two bodies.**
>
> *Aristotle*

Children

To invite children or not? If you have your own children, you can't really not invite others. If you have a big family with lots of children, it will probably be accepted that they are all going to be present. This can add considerably to the costs. You will need to ask if there is a reduction in price for children's meals at your reception venue.

Many couples feel that children will prove to be a distraction at their wedding. If you choose not to invite them, remember that you might well cause offence to those parents who feel that they should be there. Another consideration is that some guests might not be able to attend if they have no-one with whom to leave their children.

If you decide on a 'no children' rule, you will also have to decide what age you define as children. You might not want toddlers running around when speeches are being made, but 13-year-olds are a different kettle of fish! It would also not be diplomatic to leave out most children but include one or two young attendants.

Quick tip

TOO MANY?

If you find that you have more people who you want to invite than your budget will allow, you will have to be very strict about those you ask to the wedding itself. Others further out from the main set of family or friends will be more than happy simply to be invited to the evening do, if you are choosing to have one.

Animals!

For some couples, the day would not be complete without their pets being present, especially dogs. Always check with the venue to see if animals are allowed. If they are, ask someone reliable to look after them on the day. You don't want to have to go walkies in your wedding finery! It is probably best if the dog comes to meet you after the ceremony for some photos and then gets taken back home with the person you've entrusted to look after him.

STATIONERY

Once you have decided on your guest list, you will need to actually invite people. Traditionally, invitations were sent out only six weeks before the wedding day, but these days, they tend to be sent much earlier, especially if guests live a distance away and will have to make travel or hotel arrangements.

Where?

You can have wedding stationery printed by specialist suppliers. All will have huge catalogues of samples for you to choose from, ranging from traditional formal through pretty floral to quirky modern designs. You will be able to buy matching stationery covering all aspects of the wedding at the same time. There will also be examples of the wording to use.

Many high street stores and supermarkets sell blanks for you to complete yourselves. This can be a cheaper option but you might not be able to get a full selection of cards, such as Order of Service.

DIY

Card-making is a popular hobby at the moment and you can buy all the necessary items for making your own, although this is not necessarily a cheaper option.

You need to make sure your printer is up to the job for printing and the basic items can be fairly expensive. However, you will have the satisfaction of knowing that your stationery is personal to you. You can always go and look at a sample book in a specialist shop to get ideas of the wording to use!

Essentials

The most important item that you will require is a set of invitations. Don't be tempted to order one per person. You just need one per family, unless you are inviting adult children from the same house, in which case it is polite to send them a separate invitation.

You might want to choose a design that includes a reply card so that your guests have no excuse for not replying. You will need to give final numbers to your reception venue several weeks beforehand so make sure you give a date by which recipients must reply.

If you are having an evening function, you will also need invitations to this. They will have different wording and make it clear that the recipient is only invited to that function, not to the wedding itself.

More stationery

For a church wedding, you might want to have Orders of Service with the words of hymns etc. printed. If you are saving money, these are not absolutely necessary as a church will provide hymn books. Many people like to keep an Order of Service as a souvenir of the wedding.

Place cards are very important, especially if you are having a sit-down meal for your reception. Again, these can be ordered to match your set of stationery but you can also use plain white cards, available from any stationery shop. Try to get someone who is good at calligraphy to write the names on the cards.

Menus can also be useful (see Reception section).

Don't forget that you will need to send thank you letters after the wedding. Again, you can buy a set to match the rest of your stationery but you might want to produce your own (see Happy Ever After section).

Nothing like the present

These days most people expect a couple to provide a present list. This can take the form of your own printed list, or details of a store where you have set up a list. Most of the big stores will provide this service and you need to contact the one(s) you wish to deal with, as they will each have their own method. Most, these days, will set up an online list so your guests can either buy instore or via the internet.

It's a good idea to ask around and find out other people's opinions of the service provided. Some stores are better than others at getting the right presents to couples on time.

Present or money?

Many couples these days feel that they have everything they need. You might have your own flat, been living together, or it could be your second time around.

So you might think that you'd like money – possibly to go towards a large item such as a dishwasher. If so, you need to say this (tactfully) with your invitation. However, some people dislike giving money so it's a good idea to also provide a list of items. Don't be afraid to think laterally when drawing up a list. You might not need another toaster, but if you're moving from a flat to a house, what about garden tools? A camera? Or items for a joint interest? You never know, you might just get that surfboard you've always wanted!

If you definitely only want money, be aware that some people (especially the older generation) can be ill at ease, or embarrassed, by not knowing how much to give. A way round this is to tell everyone that you will have a bucket or—much prettier—a wishing well, for donations of cheques or cash. By doing this, guests can simply put in cash without disclosing the amount. You could attach a notebook so that donors could sign their names.

Your thank you letters (see later section) would then simply thank the donor for their generous gift and for sharing your day.

To have and to hold from this day forward, for better for worse, for richer for poorer, in sickness and in health, to love and to cherish till death us do part.

To have and to hold,
from this day forward;
for better, for worse,
for richer, for poorer,
in sickness and in
health, to love and
to cherish, till death
us do part;

Book of Common Prayer – Marriage Service

Church
weddings

chapter 2
Church weddings

If you decide on a church wedding, you must first check that your chosen church is registered for "the solemnization of marriage". Most Anglican churches are, but there are some non-conformist churches that are not. It does not mean that you cannot get married in them, simply that you will also need a Registrar present. A Roman Catholic Church will require a licence from the Registrar of your district.

Different faiths have different rules on who can get married in their churches, so you must make an appointment to meet with the religious leader of that faith to discuss their requirements.

First meeting

Many churches will ask you to attend marriage preparation sessions. Some may ask you to attend services on a regular basis. The vicar might well discuss the form of service that you want to use, e.g. traditional or the modern service.

The minister will also discuss the fees that you will need to pay. The standard fee will cover the publication of the banns, the marriage service and the certificate of marriage. There might well be other expenses such as the choir, bells, etc.

Anglican Church

Before you can get married, you must have Banns read in the parishes where you both live (and in the parish in which you are getting married if this is somewhere different). The Banns are an announcement of your intention to wed, and give people the opportunity to object if they so wish. They have to be read for three Sundays in the three months before your wedding date. These are usually consecutive but do not have to be.

Instead of Banns, you can apply for a common licence but you will need to discuss this with the minister.

In a queue

Check how many other weddings might be taking place on your chosen date. Popular churches get very busy, especially in the summer season, and can have up to five or six weddings on the same day, allowing only one and a quarter hours for each. This is usually adequate but you will need to tell your photographer so that he/she makes allowances and possibly arranges a second venue for photos.

If music be the food of love

Hymns are a very important part of the church service and most vicars will have a list of the most popular choices. However, you might want to choose some that are special to you. This is great, and will make the service more personal to you, providing the rest of the congregation know them too. Imagine a large church with the organ playing and only one or two people trying to sing along with an unknown hymn. Sometimes traditional ways are best!

Grand entrance

If you decide against the traditional wedding marches to walk down the aisle, make sure the organist knows the music you want played. Don't end up like the couple who requested the very romantic love song from 'Robin Hood, Prince of Thieves' ('Everything I Do' by Bryan Adams) but actually left the church to 'Robin Hood, Robin Hood, Riding through the Glen'.

Quick tip

CHOIR
Most churches have a choir and there will be a charge for it to sing at your wedding. This might be a set fee, or a fee per choir member. If this is the case, ask how many choir members are expected to attend so that you know how much you are likely to pay.

Musical extras

If you want to have some personal musical touches like a group playing, or a male voice choir, again check with your vicar before booking them. If there is another wedding booked soon after yours, there will not be time to allow this. You might have to settle for them playing or singing at your reception instead.

If you choose to book this additional entertainment, remember that you might well have to pay for their transport to the church.

Flowers

A church always looks beautiful when it is decorated with flowers for your wedding. Ask if there are any other weddings taking place on the same day as yours. If so, it might be possible to share the cost of the flowers with the other couple(s).

Although your florist will supply arrangements for the church, you might find that the person who arranges the flowers for regular church services is willing to do them. They are often very skilled and will know what sizes and shapes suit each part of the church. This usually works out a lot cheaper as well.

You might be limited to the colour and choice of flowers at certain times of the religious calendar. Again, check this well before the actual day.

Quick tip

PRACTICE MAKE PERFECT

Most churches will offer you the chance to have a rehearsal a couple of days before the wedding day. Take advantage of this so that everyone knows what they have to do on the day. Usually, the rehearsal will be for the couple, their parents, bridesmaids and best man. If the ushers have never been to the particular church before, it is a good idea if they go too so that they can see where everyone will be seated.

Practise walking and kneeling in your wedding dress. There is an art to getting up and down gracefully and you don't want to fall over in front of your guests.

" My most brilliant achievement was my ability to be able to persuade my wife to marry me. **"**

Winston Churchill

Recording the moment

When you first meet your minister, one of the questions you need to ask is about photography. Some churches will not allow photography while the ceremony is taking place. If this is the case, you will need to make this clear to your photographer/video recordist.

Quick tip

SHHHHH

A church wedding service is meant to be a serious occasion and can sometimes be spoiled by children shouting out or running around. So if you or your guests have children who will be present at the service, it is a good idea to take them to church a couple of times before the wedding day so that they get used to the building and the sense of occasion.

Large churches can be frightening to small children who have never been in one before. Also, they might not be used to sitting quietly for any length of time so an explanation of the service and the people involved would be helpful.

Fashionably late

Tradition says that the bride arrives a few minutes late. This is usually acceptable but if there are several weddings on the same day, even five minutes delay can put all the following weddings out. You don't want to be having your photos taken while the next bride is drawing up in her car.

Order of Service

After you have had photos taken as you arrive at the church, the vicar will almost certainly meet the bride and whoever is giving her away at the church door and escort them to the front of the church. If you are having a choir, they may well form a procession in front of you. The service itself will have been explained to you at either preparation sessions or the rehearsal.

Shoes

Check that all labels have been removed from the bottom of both sets of shoes. Also, the groom should check that no jokers have labelled his shoes with L and R! You don't want to hear giggles behind you when you both kneel down.

Signing the Register

After the service, the bride and groom plus witnesses will need to sign the register. This is sometimes done in view of the congregation but is often done in the vestry. To avoid confusion you will need to decide beforehand who is to go with you to sign; it is usually both sets of parents but need not be.

Procession

Once the service is over, the bride and groom will lead the guests out of church. It is customary for the bride's father to escort the groom's mother and vice versa. The best man will escort the chief bridesmaid.

If either of the mothers doesn't have a partner, it is courteous to ask a close male relative or friend to stand in so that she doesn't have to walk on her own.

Call of nature

Remember that most churches don't have toilets. Always research where the highest gravestone is because, without exception, a child will want TO GO during the service. Likewise, it's not unknown for the groom or best man to need a toilet, either because of nerves or too many 'confidence boosters' at the nearest pub beforehand. However, kind clergymen are used to this and will usually find somewhere for them.

Confetti

A shower of confetti makes a wonderful photo as you leave the wedding venue. However, check that the venue will allow it. Many churches have banned the use as it is so difficult to clear up afterwards. It is now possible to get bio-degradable confetti, which might be allowed – but you would have to make this clear to your guests before the wedding! Other options include rice and flower petals.

Rice is usually gathered up by birds and small animals after the wedding but can be very sharp if thrown straight at you. It can also be dangerous if thrown near eyes.

Dried flower petals are pretty, especially if you provide them to match your colour scheme. Florists will often provide them as part of your package, along with little cones to hand out to your guests. If you choose to do this, someone will have to be responsible for handing them to guests.

A cheaper option is to buy bags of petals and make the cones yourself from coloured paper. Again, someone will have to be responsible for handing them out. Make sure it's someone who won't wander off and leave them!

The bells, the bells!

The sound of the bells ringing is linked with weddings. Like the choir, the cost of the bell ringers will not be included in the basic price for the service. If the church has a peal of bells, they will usually ring out as the bride arrives, then as the couple leave the church, and for some time afterwards.

Bells can be very loud. If you are having a video made of the day, check with your video company that the noise of the bells can be faded or it will overpower the rest of the sounds and conversation.

A little snack!

There is often quite a long time between the start of a wedding and sitting down to eat at the reception. This is especially so if guests have had to travel some distance even before the ceremony starts. Children can become very bad-tempered and disruptive if they are hungry so you could provide a few boxes of biscuits or packets of crisps and cartons of drinks with straws to keep them going. They can be produced from a car's boot by a willing helper. You'll probably find that it won't only be children who take advantage, especially if there are some drinks on a hot day. It won't cost very much and can make a lot of difference to frayed tempers!

Marriage –
the beautiful
blending of two lives,
two hearts, two loves.

Anon

Civil weddings

chapter 3
Civil weddings

A civil wedding is one that is held in a Register Office or an approved venue. Marriages cannot be held out of doors in England and Wales. You can find a list of approved venues in your area from your local Register Office or on **www.gro.gov.uk.**

Many Register Offices now operate an appointments system so always ring first rather than just turning up to try to book your wedding.

For either a wedding in the Register Office or at an approved venue, you need to give 'notice of marriage' at least 15 days before your chosen date, with evidence of name, address, marital status, and nationality. Both of you need to attend the Register Office, no-one else can do it for you. You need to have resided in the area for at least 7 days prior to giving notice. Once you have done this, your notice of marriage will be displayed on a notice board in the Register Office for anyone to view.

Registering for a marriage

You will need to give the Superintendent Registrar: Your name. Proof of age. Proof of residency, e.g. passport.

If you have been married before, you will also need: Divorce Decree Absolute or Death Certificate of your former spouse.

Booking ahead

A notice of marriage lasts for one year so that is the maximum time ahead that you can book the Register Office. You will almost certainly be able to book an approved venue further in advance and some Registrars will allow you to book their services over a year ahead for such a venue. However, you will still not be able to take out the notice of marriage more than one year before your wedding. Your venue will be able to advise on the procedure for that. Popular venues get booked very early so it is a good idea to get your venue booked, even if you can't confirm the time until you've been in touch with the Registrar.

Quick tip

SIZE MATTERS

If you decide to get married in a Register Office or an hotel, always check how many guests can be accommodated. It is no good booking a room that will only hold 30 people if you know you want at least 100 guests. Most hotel ceremony rooms and Register Offices are far smaller than churches. Some venues will limit the number of bridesmaids that they will allow because of the space available at the front of the wedding room. This might be worth checking if you want to have several attendants.

The ceremony

The civil marriage ceremony will be the same whether you are in a Register Office or an approved venue.

REGISTER OFFICE

The size and location of these varies enormously. Some are in beautiful buildings, others in council offices. However, nowadays, ceremonies in these offices have lost their hole-in-a-corner, rushed-wedding reputation and are generally dignified occasions with many personal touches.

You might find that your local office offers a range of ceremonies. The cheapest option will be a basic ceremony with the minimum requirements in the presence of two witnesses. Some offices might offer several longer (and more expensive) ceremonies and your chance to write your own vows etc.

Personal touch

Although you might be able to choose the vows, words, and music at your ceremony, you should be aware that they must be non-religious. Also, they must not be edited to leave out any religious references. Many Registrars will have a book with a choice of suggested words and readings. However, if you have a special piece that you would like to use, you should make sure that it is approved by the Superintendent Registrar at least seven days before the ceremony. You should give both the names of the author and the person who is going to read the piece. This gives time for it to be included in the ceremony.

The law does not require you to exchange rings, but most couples do, so you will need to discuss the promises that will be made at that point in the ceremony.

Good timing

Register Offices can be very busy places, especially on a Saturday. They might well have weddings happening every 15 minutes (if they have 2 wedding rooms). One late wedding will hold up everyone else's so make sure that you and your guests are on time. This is not a place for the bride being traditionally late. The Registrar can cancel your wedding if you are not there at the proper time.

Parking is sometimes limited at Register Offices so advise your guests to leave extra time if they need to park elsewhere. If they have never visited the town before, it is a good idea to provide a map of the area with the nearest car parks marked – and an idea of the cost so they can have the right change ready.

APPROVED VENUES

Approved venues can range from stately homes to football stadia, and facilities will vary from place to place. Always go and view the ones that you like the look of and speak to the wedding co-ordinator. Many will arrange wedding fairs throughout the year. This gives you a good chance to see the facilities set up for a wedding.

Most, but not all, will offer a marriage ceremony and reception package. Some only offer the room for the ceremony and you will have to find another venue for your reception.

NOT A CHEAP OPTION

Don't automatically assume that a civil wedding is a cheaper option than a church one. If you decide to get married in an hotel, you will probably be quoted an all-inclusive price. This might seem like a good deal but almost certainly doesn't include the Registrar's fee. You will have to pay for the Registrar to attend the ceremony and this will be far higher than the fee you would pay at the actual Register Office, and can add to your overall budget.

Co-ordination

Most approved venues will have a wedding co-ordinator whose job is to arrange the wedding exactly as you wish (see Receptions).

Always ask what is provided in the ceremony room, and how it will be arranged. Don't assume that there will be an arrangement of flowers, as this is not always the case. You might have to provide these yourself if you wish to have them.

Some venues will have a selection of music that will be played while guests are waiting, and for you to enter and leave the room. If you have favourite music, you will need to provide this in advance.

LEAVING THE COUNTRY

You might decide that you want to leave everything behind and escape to somewhere exotic to get married. This can be a wonderful idea and surely the most romantic wedding photos are those taken on a golden beach!

Making it legal

Vows taken on a moonlit beach when you're on holiday might be romantic but might not be legal. It is important that you know what the law is. If you want to get married abroad, you can make all the arrangements yourself, using the internet to check on the laws for individual countries. **However, m**any tour operators now offer wedding packages. This means that they will make sure the marriage will be legal in this country as well as the foreign country. Most well-known names are reliable companies but things can still go wrong. It is just as important, if not more so, to take out wedding insurance. Always double check the documents that you need to take with you.

Check first

Before you make your booking, ask the travel company if they can put you in touch with couples who have got married in the same resort, or check unbiased websites for views of the resorts.

Weather

Research the average weather conditions at your chosen time of year. You don't want to spend all your money on a luxury wedding in the Caribbean, only to find that it is hurricane season and that your wedding is cancelled due to the storms.

Who to take?

If you want the wedding to be just for the two of you, that's fine. However, many couples decide to make the occasion a family holiday and take parents, children, and attendants with them. If this is what you want to do, always discuss it with the family first. Make sure who is paying for what and check that everyone can afford to go.

Think about the family and decide if they are going to be able to get along with each other for a whole holiday. People who can get on with each other for a day at home might not manage two weeks together. You don't want your wedding spoiled by squabbling relatives.

Dressing-up

There are tips for clothes for weddings abroad in the Clothes for All section.

Quick tip

AND AFTER?

Many couples choose to have a reception or party after they return so that the family and friends who were not able to attend the wedding can celebrate. This can be quite an informal affair and can be arranged like the evening occasions in the Reception section. Apart from seeing all your family and friends, it's a good opportunity to wear the wedding dress again!

Your wedding day is like a fairy tale; you've had to kiss a lot of frogs to find your prince.

Anon

Getting a good reception

chapter 4
Getting a good reception

In Roman times a marriage wasn't legal until the bride and groom had eaten bread together! Perhaps you have dreamed of holding your reception at a specific venue ever since you were a child, however if you haven't a clue where to go, it pays to do your research. Prices, food, standards of service, and extras vary enormously.

The main venues for receptions are: hotels and country clubs, restaurants, pubs, social clubs, or your own home – indoors or in a marquee.

Variety of choice

Most hotels and country clubs offer wedding packages. These tend to include the meal, an evening function and, often, a night in the wedding suite. They usually have a choice of function room depending on the number of guests, or might provide a marquee for summer weddings. Most will have a wedding co-ordinator to help you make your arrangements.

Restaurants might offer wedding packages, and can be ideal for the smaller wedding. Remember though, that they might not give you sole use of the room but remain open for other clients. This can be a bit inhibiting if you decide to have speeches and toasts.

Other venues

Pubs and social clubs – these vary in quality. Some will provide catering; others will provide a room but expect you to provide the catering.

Home – this choice can be ideal if you are on a budget, and have a house that is big enough to hold all your guests.

Marquee – this can be a very romantic choice if you have a large garden or decent field but there are several things to take into account (see separate section later).

Careful calculations

Always have a budget in mind when selecting your reception venue. If your budget is £4,000 and the venue of your dreams charges £100 a head, it means that you can only have 40 people at your reception. If you want to have 100 people there, you will have to find somewhere that only charges £40 a head.

If you need specialist caterers (e.g. Kosher) not in your area, you will have to add the cost of transport for the catering staff.

Quick tip

YOU COUNT TOO!
Don't forget to add in the number of the wedding party – it's amazing how many couples forget to count themselves when calculating costs. The main party might have at least eight people: bride and groom, four parents, best man, and chief bridesmaid, all of whom have to be included in the total costs.

How to work out your costs
if booking a wedding package

Add together:

- Cost of meal x number of guests.

- Cost of drinks package x number of guests.

- Cost of evening buffet x number of guests (if applicable).

- Hire of room.

- Hire of Toastmaster.

- Hire of cake stand and knife.

- Cost of flowers for tables.

- Cost of other room decorations (e.g. balloons, sprinkles).

- Cost of live music and/or DJ or disco.

- Additional cost for using photographer at reception (if applicable)

- If at a hotel – cost of bedrooms for bride & groom and parents (if staying over)

- VAT if not already included in prices.

Make sure there is someone to pick you up off the floor when you see the final total!

Research

When you go to check out any venue, there are several things to look out for.

If there is a wedding co-ordinator, see if he/she makes you feel welcome at your initial visit. If not, he might have the same attitude on your wedding day.

If you are shown a very large function room, check if it can be divided in half so that the venue can hold two receptions on the same day. This doesn't necessarily create a problem, but some room dividers are not soundproofed. You don't want the noise from another wedding to spoil your speeches.

Ask if there is likely to be more than one wedding at the venue on the day. Again, this needn't be a problem, and it often happens at large popular venues. However, you need to make sure that both wedding parties are not arriving at the same time, especially if you want to use an imposing entrance or pretty garden for photos.

Food glorious food

Most venues will provide a variety of menus for you to choose from. These will usually be priced per head and will vary depending on the choice of food on offer. If you have your own ideas, most venues will be happy to discuss your requirements and give you a quote.

Again, many venues will quote for a drinks package on top of the food menu, usually consisting of a drink on arrival, wine with the meal and a glass of bubbly for the toast. You are under no obligation to purchase this option; you might want guests to buy their own drinks, or you might just want to provide a drink for a toast. If you want to provide your own wine or champagne, ask if this is possible and what the venue charges for corkage, i.e. a cost per bottle for using your own. There might be an additional cost for coffee served after the meal.

What to eat?

This will obviously be a very personal choice. The easiest option is to have just one choice for everyone, although you should ensure that anyone with a special diet is catered for. Many venues nowadays will allow you to have two or three choices for each course. This makes it nicer for the guests but you will have the added responsibility of ensuring that everyone makes a choice by the required date.

The easiest way to do this is to send out a tick-list menu with your invitations. Hopefully, the guests will then be able to send it back with their reply. Make sure you send enough tick-lists for each member of the family and give a deadline for the replies. As your replies come back, keep a list of the chosen items so that you can give it to the venue on the requested date.

Quick tip

A QUICK REMINDER
If you have asked guests to choose their menu beforehand, it is a good idea to produce small menus to put by each place setting. Guests don't always remember what they have chosen and this saves any awkward arguments with the serving staff.

Pubs and social clubs

Most social clubs, and some pubs, have a function room that they hire out for special occasions. They vary in price and some clubs will only allow a room to be booked by a member. Always have a look at the room before you book as they vary in quality.

If using a function room, check that a bar is provided in the same room. You don't want your guests to wander into another area and stop there to drink, especially if it's a Saturday and there's football on the TV in the bar!

Most social clubs will offer catering, or will know of an outside caterer. Again, it is worth checking their menu as these, too, vary from excellent to poor. Word of mouth is a good test of the quality of the food.

If you want to do your own catering, check that this is acceptable – and see the section on catering at home. Some clubs will not allow this.

Restaurants

If you decide to have your reception meal in a restaurant, ask if they are willing to let you have the whole room for the occasion. Some will be willing to do this for a lunchtime/early afternoon reception but will need you to be out of the venue so that they can prepare for the evening bookings. It is important that you know this so that your guests can be warned in advance that they will have to leave.

If the restaurant offers a wedding package, the tips are the same as for hotels and country clubs. However, some restaurants will expect you to do the organisation yourself.

Menu

It is easier if you choose the main courses from the restaurant menu beforehand, rather than allowing people free choice (unless there are only about eight of you). This makes it easier for the restaurant staff to serve all the guests at the same time, and also allows you to keep control of the budget. You can also choose in advance the wine that you would like to be served. Again, this prevents any large bills for costly champagne that someone has ordered on the spur of the moment!

AT HOME

If you are having a small wedding, or you have a very large house, a reception in your own home can be an attractive proposition. It will prove to be a lot cheaper and will also be a very personal occasion.

DELEGATE

Although you might well have done all the preparation yourselves, you will need to delegate on the day itself. Make sure you ask reliable people to help and that they know what they are expected to do. You want to enjoy the day, not worry about whether people have enough to eat. You don't want to be cutting up quiches or pouring wine in your wedding finery.

All the facilities

Your guests will need somewhere to leave coats so make sure you've tidied one of the bedrooms! Work out if you have enough toilets for the number of guests. If you have more than one loo, it is a good idea to label them for Ladies and Gentlemen, making sure the Ladies' has a good mirror. A portaloo can be hired at a reasonable price if you have a suitable place to site it.

If you haven't got enough plates and glasses for everyone, you can hire matching sets from specialist hire shops, or many off-licences (and some supermarkets) will do glass hire at a low cost. You can also buy pretty disposable plates – a good idea to cut down on clearing up afterwards. Wedding serviettes and table decorations are available at specialist shops and many supermarkets.

Food – call in the professionals

There are many small catering companies which specialise in providing buffet (or sit-down) meals for special occasions. The best way to find one is by word of mouth but you can also look in Yellow Pages etc. If you haven't tasted the finished result for yourself, don't be afraid to ask for some samples of the type of food provided. It is important that you get what you want.

Always check what a caterer provides or needs. Most will bring serving trays, but you might need to provide tablecloths etc.

Always arrange what time the caterers are going to arrive at your venue. If you have to leave for your wedding before they are due to get there, arrange for someone to be available to let them in.

The DIY buffet

This is where a freezer comes into its own. Most supermarkets and freezer stores now sell ranges of party food, much of which can simply be defrosted ready to serve on attractive plates.

If you have access to a cash and carry warehouse, you can buy catering packs of cold meat, cheese, etc. However, remember that some prices will be exclusive of VAT which will be added at the checkout, so they might not be as cheap as they appear. Supermarkets will be happy to sell large amounts to you, especially if you order in advance. Some also sell trays of ready made sandwiches and nibbles.

"Spouse: someone who'll stand by you through all the trouble you wouldn't have had if you'd stayed single."

Anon

Cheers!

The bill for drinks can add considerably to the cost of a reception and, unlike a party, it's not really polite to ask all your guests to bring a bottle. Look out for BOGOF (Buy-One-Get-One-Free) offers at supermarkets or buy your bottles of wine a few at time when there are special deals on. They won't go off and you just need somewhere to store them where they won't get drunk in advance!

Champagne is expensive and you can get sparkling wines at a fraction of the cost. Many off-licences will let you buy drink on a sale-or-return basis.

Don't forget to have a good selection of non-alcoholic drinks on offer, especially if you have guests who are driving. Children might be happy with squash or juice, but try to get some more sophisticated ones for your adult non-drinkers.

Quick tip

HOT STUFF!

If you want to serve a hot buffet, most of the ranges of party food from the freezer are ready to pop on the oven. However, timings are important if everything is to be on the table at the same time and domestic ovens tend to be limited in the number of trays that can be put in at one time. If you are on good terms with your neighbours, ask if they would mind cooking a few trays for you so that your helpers can get everything out at the right time.

Alternatives!

If you're having an informal reception, especially if it's outdoors, try thinking of alternatives to the normal menu. Fish and chip shops and other take-aways will often deliver large quantities, or you could book a hog roast for a barbeque.

For real fun, why not book the local ice-cream company and get them to bring their van so that all your guests can have ice-creams for afters? They will all certainly remember the day!

Keeping cool

You'll probably need your fridge for the food, so you'll have to think of other ways of keeping the beer and wine cool. Many supermarkets sell bags of ice, so you could fill a clean bin with ice and pop all the cans and bottles into it. If you go camping, or have friends who do, you might have an electric cool box – the type that plugs into a car cigarette lighter. These usually have mains adaptors and will keep drinks very cold.

MARQUEE

If you, or a good family friend, have a large garden or field, a hired marquee can be an attractive alternative to a hotel for your reception. However, there are several points to take into consideration.

Size and requirements

The first requirement, but one often overlooked, is that your area needs to be relatively flat! If you are using a field, you also want to check that no animals have been using it for some time before the wedding date. Animal poo is not ideal at a wedding!

The formula for working out the size of a marquee is to allow 20 sq.ft.(2 sq.m) per person. This will allow enough room for tables and chairs, bar area, and a dance area. There also needs to be some space around the proposed area for the marquee company to work in whilst erecting it. Most companies will also provide a smaller tent for the catering, so space for this also needs to be calculated, as does room for the generators required providing electricity. These generators will also need access to electricity from the nearest building.

The British weather can be very uncertain so a covered passageway from the house is a good idea. The outside of marquees is usually ivory and most reputable companies will be able to provide linings to complement your colour scheme. There is also a range of floorings; matting is the cheapest, but you can also have wooden floors or, the most expensive, carpeting. Heating will also usually be arranged. You will need to allow between 2½ and 3 days for the erection of a large marquee.

Spending a penny

Unless you have a large house with loads of toilets, facilities will have to made available for guests. Most marquee hire companies will be able to provide (or recommend another company to provide) portaloos. These are no longer the blue huts found on building sites, but luxury trailers with flushing toilets, wash basins and all the facilities found in a good hotel.

Catering

See the suggestions for catering at home or in a hired hall.

Happiness is being married to your best friend.

Anon

Eat, drink & be merry

chapter 5

chapter 5
Eat, drink & be merry

The wedding cake originated with small cakes baked from flour and fruits to encourage fertility! Nowadays, it is considered lucky for the bride and groom to make the first cut in the cake together.

Once you've chosen your reception venue and the menu, it's time to think about the reception itself.

Getting organised

If you have a wedding coordinator, she should be there to greet you as you arrive at the venue. She will also tell everyone where they need to be – and when. If not, it will be the Best Man's job to organise your guests. This will start with arranging the receiving line.

Receiving line

Many couples think that a 'receiving line' is rather old-fashioned. However, it can be a very good idea, especially if you each have guests from various parts of the country who have never met each other's families. It gives time to put faces to names.

It need not be too formal with a straight line, but the bride and groom plus both sets of parents can greet the guests as they arrive. They can be introduced to the other family with a brief handshake or kiss.

Tables

Your wedding co-ordinator will advise as to the arrangement that suits the room the best. The two main ways are to have a horseshoe with a top table and two long wings, or a top table plus several round tables, each seating six to ten guests.

The horseshoe arrangement means that everyone can see the top table, however round tables tend to be more informal so that guests can chat to each other. It is not advisable to have a round top table as the view of the bride and groom will be obscured.

The traditional seating plan for the top table (looking towards the table) is:

Chief B'maid: Groom's Father: Bride's Mother: Groom: Bride: Bride's Father: Groom's Mother: Best Man

However, this can be quite flexible, especially where parents have been divorced and have new partners. Rather than stick to tradition and cause bad feeling, it is better to be more tactful and include new partners on the top table. Ushers and other bridesmaids can also be included if you wish.

It is customary to seat closer relatives and friends nearer to the top table and others further away. It is also customary to alternate male and female guests if possible. On round tables, partners can sit next to each other; on long tables it is usual to seat them opposite each other. It is wise to keep young children near to their parents.

Speech time!

Making a speech seems to be the one thing that people are most afraid of. Unless the bride has decided to make a speech, her nerve-wracking part is over once the couple get to the reception. However, the groom and best man have the thought of it hanging over them for the whole time.

You might have booked a toastmaster or your wedding co-ordinator might act as one at your chosen venue. If so, he/she will announce the speeches at the right time. This will be after the main meal, when your guests should be nicely relaxed.

However, some couples choose to have the speeches before the meal so that the nerves are out of the way. If you want to do this, you need to let the venue know your plans so that catering times can be arranged to suit you. You don't want the soup arriving in the middle of the best man's jokes.

You might want someone to say a Grace before the meal. This might be the toastmaster or the best man. Graces are generally very short.

A few examples:

For what we are about to receive, may the Lord make us truly thankful.

We thank you Lord for happy hearts
For rain and sunny weather
We thank you for the food we eat
And that we are together.
Amen.

Who says what?

There is a traditional order for the speeches.

The first should be made by either the bride's father or someone who is taking his place for the day. His job is to make a toast to wish the bride and groom happiness and luck.

This speech can simply be that — a toast. However, he might wish to say something about the bride growing up and welcoming the groom into the family. Another nice touch is to mention the happiness that he's had in his own marriage to the bride's mother.

Toasts

These can be very straightforward:

'Ladies and Gentlemen: I ask you to stand and toast x and y, the bride and groom.'

The second speech is a response by the groom, thanking the father for his good wishes. He should then make a toast to the bridesmaids to thank them for their help throughout the day, and for looking so beautiful. It is also a welcome touch to thank everyone who has helped in the preparation for the day.

It is usual to give small gifts to the bridesmaids and best man. If this has not already been done (e.g. you might have chosen an item of jewellery to be worn on the day) this is the time to present them. Some couples also like to give flowers to both mothers as a thank you for their help.

The third speech is the one that people look forward to most of all — the best man's speech. He should respond on behalf of the bridesmaids, and then make his speech. When telegrams used to be sent, he also read those. Although these are no longer around, it is usually appreciated if a few cards are read out with messages from guests who are unable to attend.

If the bride wishes to make a speech, she should do it when the others have been made.

Calming the nerves

Everyone gets nervous at the thought of making a speech but there are certain techniques you can do to calm the nerves.

Whatever else you do, don't get drunk! One drink to steady the nerves is OK but after that, anything could happen. You don't want to stray from that carefully prepared speech and start insulting the new in-laws!

Remember that the people in front of you are your family and friends. They are not there to judge your performance as an orator but to join in with wishing you all well.

Be prepared

Preparation is the key to a successful speech. Unless it is something you do everyday, don't expect to be able to wing it on the day. There are plenty of books and websites with examples of speeches but try to make them as personal as possible.

It's not a good idea to write a speech out word for word as that will make it sound stilted. Work out what you are going to say, write key points down on cards, then practise on your own until you are confident. Fix the cards together in the right order so that you don't end up getting confused.

KEEP IT SIMPLE
No-one is expecting an Oscar acceptance speech that rambles on for hours so remember the saying "short and sweet". Be sincere in what you say; this goes down far better than attempts at bad jokes.

Best man's speech

It is usual for the best man's speech to be humorous but this doesn't mean risqué jokes. If he's known the groom for many years, there are bound to be some funny stories from his youth that can be put in. However, stories about his exploits with other women are definitely not on the menu!

There are many books on sale with formatted speeches, and websites that offer to write the speech for you. These are great to get some hints and ideas but the home-written one is always the most sincere.

On the tables

Always check with the venue as to what they provide on the table. Some will provide floral arrangements and use napkins to match your colour scheme. Others will charge extra for flowers and you might want to provide your own.

The cake

The wedding cake is an important centrepiece of the reception. Traditionally, the cake was a three-tier fruit cake, iced with flowers and favours. Nowadays, there is far more choice of designs from pretty floral through zany, to ones showing the couple's interests.

Many people do not like the traditional fruit cake, so alternatives could be chocolate cake, or plain Madeira. You can also have different tiers in different types of cake. A fruit cake is heavy and will cut up into many pieces, so some people opt to have that for the bottom tier.

If you are going to save the top tier for a christening cake, fruit cake will store for the longest time.

Where to get your cake?

Although there are shops that design and sell cakes, you will also find that many cake makers are single-person businesses, with the owner baking and decorating in their own homes. They are often very skilled craftsmen and you will get an individually-designed cake.

Most will have a portfolio of photos of their finished items but try to see a real one. Wedding fairs are good places to see finished cakes, and most makers will have a piece of cake for you to try before you order.

Some cakes need specially shaped stands so check if the maker hires or lends a cake stand with the cake.

Take time

Wedding cakes to your own design are not things that can be rushed out at the last minute. Although some professionals will keep ready made cakes in store, they still take a time to decorate so order several months in advance of the day.

Bake it yourself

You might well have a family recipe that is traditionally used for family occasions. If you do, but don't have a family member or friend who is skilled at decoration, it is worth asking a professional if they would decorate a cake you provide. However, many will not do this as they have horror stories of being asked to make something beautiful from a cake which has sunk in the middle, or is burnt on the edges.

Another idea is to ask your local adult education centre if they have a cake-decorating or sugarcraft class. You will often find someone who is very skilled and delighted to have another cake on which to show off their skills.

Ready made

You can also buy cakes ready made, and this will prove to be a cheaper option. Many supermarkets now sell plain iced cakes in a variety of sizes so you can build up as many tiers as you want. You can then decorate them to your colour scheme with small favours and fresh or silk flowers. There are many cake-top decorations to buy in any store that sells cake decorating tools and materials.

That sinking feeling

If you are building your own tiers, you will need a set of pillars for each tier. These are hollow and a good idea is to push a piece of wooden dowelling down through the cake and up through the pillar. This then takes the weight of the upper tier, otherwise the pillars might start to sink through the icing.

Quick tip

ON SHOW

Always check if the reception venue lends a cake stand and knife to cut the cake. Some will charge extra for the privilege! When you see the reception room, ask where the cake will be sited. Some will put it in the middle of the top table, but a small table to one side will often be more convenient and save it being bumped or, even worse, knocked over.

Getting things back

After the photo of the cake being cut has been taken, it is usually whisked away to be cut into small pieces for the guests. Make sure that someone checks that the decorations are returned to you. In the excitement of the day, it might be the last thing you'd think of, but many brides have been upset to find that decorations have been thrown away by kitchen staff.

This can also apply to your table decorations. If you want to keep the flowers, you will need to make sure that someone is responsible for taking them home for you.

"One of the best
things about marriage
is that it gets young
people to bed at
a decent hour.

M.M. Musselman

FRILLS AND FAVOURS

A trip round any wedding fair will show you that there is a vast array of extras you can add to your wedding reception.

Personal theme

One idea is to have your tables themed to match the interests of the bride and groom. Keen surfers might like to use a beach theme with shells holding the name cards; football fans might want to use their team colours.

You might also want to theme your wedding to the time of year. Christmas or St. Valentine's weddings might be obvious but Easter ones could have daffodils and Easter eggs on the tables. Autumn leaves also look beautiful for October weddings.

Favours

The original favours originated in Europe with five sugared almonds, symbolising Health, Wealth, Fertility, Long life and Happiness – and what more could anyone wish for a newly-married couple?

If you want to stay with almonds or other sweets (love hearts, chocolates) there are many styles of container to choose. Some are plain ivory, with the possibility of a coloured flower decoration, but there are also many more complicated shapes to choose. You can also push the boat out and have porcelain containers with details of your wedding printed on them. Don't forget though, that people often forget to pick them up and take them home. They could be costly litter left on your tables. There are also children's boxes available to amuse your younger guests.

Crafty plan

To save money you can buy flat boxes to make up yourself and decorate to match your colour scheme, or cut circles of net and tie up with a pretty ribbon. Make sure you have enough sweets to fill them. You don't get many sugared almonds in a 100g bag! A cash-and-carry can sell you large jars of sweets.

Other ideas

If you want to provide a small favour for your guests, but not sweets, there are many other suggestions.

Lottery scratch cards make a fun gift, especially if they are packed into pretty cards to match your scheme. They also give the chance of someone becoming rich at your wedding (they could then offer to pay the bills for you!).

Some couples like to give separate male and female gifts. If you want to push the boat out, men might like an engraved miniature of spirits – these can be engraved with your initials or the date of the wedding.

Balloons

Almost any shape made in balloons can be provided by a specialist company, in almost any colour to suit your scheme. Arches can look lovely at a civil ceremony or over a top table at a reception. Many couples like to have an arrangement of balloons floating above each table.

It can be tempting to think you can do your own balloons but there are a few drawbacks. Most sold in general shops tend to be smaller than those provided by specialist suppliers.

This means that they have shorter flying time so need to be blown up on the day of the wedding. Tanks of helium can be bought to do this, but you will have to delegate the job to a few reliable people. It is just not on for the bride to have to blow balloons up as well as all the other things on her list.

If going to a specialist company, ask when they balloons will be blown up. They should guarantee to blow them on the morning of the wedding so you don't end up with droopy latex!

Pearlised balloons look nicer than ordinary ones for weddings.

Quick tip

DANGER!

Helium balloons are not flammable but warn your guests not to try the old trick of making the voice get higher by inhaling the gas. Helium can kill and is especially dangerous for anyone with asthma.

EVENING RECEPTION

The evening reception will almost certainly be a far more informal occasion than the earlier reception. It is usually an opportunity to invite guests that couldn't be accommodated at the wedding itself. Your invitations should specify the end time so that guests know what time to arrange taxis etc.

Most venues will be able to recommend a disco.

Peace and quiet

Weddings are usually times when people can catch up with family news. Discos can be very loud and many guests will appreciate somewhere quiet to sit and chat. Check with your venue to see if you have the use of more than the main room.

Numbers

Check with your venue how strict they are with numbers for catering. Some will be fairly relaxed and allow you to book a buffet for 100, even if a few extra turn up. Others are rather stricter and will have someone to count the number of guests on arrival. They will then charge you for the actual number and this could be an unpleasant surprise especially if gate-crashers arrive!

The first dance

The bride and groom will be expected to dance the first dance of the evening. You might love dancing and have no worries about this, but you could also surprise your guests with a 'Strictly Come Dancing' demonstration. Many ballroom dance schools offer wedding dance classes so you can amaze everyone with your twirls.

Make a bet!

Casinos can be hired to entertain your guests, usually roulette and blackjack. Croupiers will set them up for you and run the games. They are generally played with provided chips – you don't have to worry that your guests are going to lose their shirts!

Chocolate heaven

Chocolate fountains can now be bought for you to set up yourself but they tend to be rather small, really only intended for home and party use. For a large reception, it is better to hire a bigger model. This will ensure that the machine is set up and filled by the hire company. They will also provide the dips, sticks, and a supply of serviettes. Many will also provide a 'chocolate lifeguard' who will look after the machine all evening, making sure that children (and chocoholics) don't get carried away.

Wine on tap

A champagne fountain need not have sparkling wine, but looks better with some sort of bubbly. They generally take 16 litres of wine and you will need to provide your choice for this.

Out with a bang!

If you really want to finish the evening off with a dramatic flourish, you can have a firework display. You can now buy fireworks throughout the year, but if you decide on a DIY display, make sure you have someone reliable in charge. Even just a few glasses of bubbly can affect the most sensible of people. In addition, you need to make sure there is an adequate area available and that you have permission from your venue.

This is one occasion when it is better, even though more costly, to rely on the professionals. Companies will set up and fire the display for you so all you have to do is enjoy the sparkling display. ENJOY YOURSELVES!!!

When you meet someone who can cook and do housework – don't hesitate a minute – marry him!

Anon

Dancing
attendance

chapter 6
Dancing attendance

Bridesmaids were originally friends of the bride who dressed in equally fine gowns to confuse the evil spirits!

Giving the bride away

Traditionally this is the job of the bride's father but there might be circumstances where this is not possible. Another close male relative would usually be the next choice, but there is no reason why it has to be a man. Many brides choose to have their mother escort them down the aisle, especially if her father has died, or if Mum has brought her up on her own. If you have children, you might like your son or daughter to escort you. The escort should walk on the bride's left as they enter the venue.

BRIDESMAIDS

Who to choose

Remember, the job of the bridesmaid is exactly that – the bride's maid. They are there to help you. Long gone are the days when the maid had to help bath the bride and dress her hair, but it really is useful to have a chief bridesmaid who will support you, calm your nerves, and fade into the background if necessary. Don't choose anyone who is more interested in pulling the best man or hoping the photographer will pick her as his next model.

How many?

You might be from a big family and will offend loads of people by not asking them to be an attendant – especially if there are lots of little girls in the family, all desperate to be a flower girl. There are always cases of 'having to have Cousin X, because cousin Y is being a pageboy'. However, remember, it is still YOUR wedding and up to you. It's no good having nine attendants if you don't know half of them very well. If you only want one, then just have one. OK, so you'll have to explain to all the disappointed families but better that than being worried all day because the attendants are arguing with each other.

Some civil venues limit the number of attendants you are permitted. Always check this before asking children to be bridesmaids, otherwise you might have some very disappointed little faces.

Little darlings

If you're planning a wedding up to two years ahead, bear in mind that children grow up. The angelic little boy with blond curls that you want as a page boy now might well be a gap-toothed demon in two years' time. And that sweet little girl could grow into a spoilt little madam who will stamp her foot at the slightest provocation.

Don't get carried away choosing the dresses straight away. A pretty bridesmaid's dress that suits a 10-year-old now, will almost certainly not suit her in two years' time when she might be a different shape altogether. Wait until you know the approximate sizes.

Chief bridesmaid

The chief bridesmaid will be very important to the smooth running of your wedding. She is there to provide support in any way possible, although telling you to change your mind isn't possibly the best way of doing it!

She should be at the bride's house as early as possible so that any last minute hitches can be ironed out with the minimum of fuss. She will probably go to the hairdresser with you and will certainly help you to get dressed.

Other adult bridesmaids

These don't really have an allocated role to play except for making sure your train doesn't get dirty on the way into the ceremony. They can concentrate on looking good. However, if you also have child bridesmaids, it is a good idea to delegate one of your older bridesmaids to be in charge of them. She can make sure that they all get into the right car, that they don't run off anywhere before entering the venue, and generally make sure they don't make a nuisance of themselves.

Quick tip

CHILD ATTENDANTS

If you are having child attendants, always make sure they know what they are going to do. It is unlikely that they will be able to help you in any way, but they will look pretty!

Best man

The best man's job is to support the groom, both in the wedding preparations and on The Day itself. Traditionally it was usual for the groom to ask his brother to support him on the day, but this does not have to be the case. Of course, the job usually associated with the best man is making his speech at the reception and whilst it might be tempting to ask someone who you know will be the life and soul of the party, this is not always a good idea. You need someone who will take his job seriously and keep everything under control. You don't want to be worried on the day by little things that can be sorted out easily by a capable best man.

Although the name implies that the best man should be male, there is not a rule that says it has to be. Some grooms will choose to have a close female relative or friend to support them on the day.

What does the best man do?

His main job is to make sure that the groom arrives at the venue in plenty of time. The journey might include a swift drink at a local pub, but it is the best man's job to make sure that the groom doesn't linger there, or even, worse, arrive at the venue worse for wear.

His other, very important, job is to produce the ring(s) at the right moment in the ceremony. He needs to check that he has them with him before leaving for the venue. It is a good idea to keep them in a box or jewellery bag in his pocket so that there's no chance of them slipping down through a hole in the lining and making him search his suit in front of all the guests.

He is also responsible for making sure that all the fees are paid at the wedding venue and ensuring that everyone is able to get from the venue to the reception if necessary.

The best man should be responsible for checking that all the hired suits for the male members of the wedding party have arrived in good order. He might need to collect them from the hire shop so make sure that he knows who is wearing what, and where they should go to – don't leave bride's dad's suit at the groom's house!

Traditionally, the best man is responsible for ordering the bride's flowers and those for the mothers etc. but nowadays most brides prefer to choose and order their own.

He might also, if there is no wedding co-ordinator or toastmaster, be the person to announce the speeches and cake-cutting.

Ushers

The ushers' job is to provide help to the groom and best man. Usually this is to show people to their seats, especially at a church wedding, and to make sure that everyone has transport to the reception afterwards. This means that they need to be reliable, turn up in plenty of time and not sit in the pub until five minutes before the wedding.

Traditionally, the ushers are male but, like most things these days, there is no rule that says they must be and there is no reason why ladies cannot act as ushers.

The number of ushers will depend on the size of the wedding. If there are up to around 70 guests, two will probably be enough. Although, traditionally, the ushers were friends of the groom, nowadays it is helpful if at least one is from the bride's side of the family so that he can recognise members of the family as they arrive.

Quick tip

TOKENS OF APPRECIATION
It is usual for the couple to give a small gift to the attendants to thank them for their help. If you choose to give the bridesmaids the traditional jewellery, or cufflinks to the best man and ushers, it is a good idea to give them on the morning of the wedding so that they can wear them. Otherwise they should be given at the time of the groom's speech when he thanks them. Other ideas for gifts are engraved glasses for adult helpers and soft toys for the children.

Other useful helpers

Unfortunately, we can never rely on the British weather to provide a hot sunny day. It is a good idea to have one or two helpers with umbrellas, especially if there is long walk from the cars to the venue. This could be done by the ushers, but sometimes they are busy inside the venue and not watching for arrivals outside.

Stag and Hen nights

Traditionally it is the best man's and the chief bridesmaid's job to organise the Stag and Hen Nights. These can be a simple as a night out at the local pub or as extravagant as a weekend away. Whatever happens, they should not take place on the night before the wedding. After going to all the expense of a wedding, both bride and groom want to be able to remember the day, not have it pass in a hungover state.

After all the stress of preparing for a wedding, brides might well appreciate a day or two at a spa with a few of her best friends (and possibly Mum). Or how about a weekend seeing the sights in New York? The more budget-conscious might like an evening in with a make-up party and a few bottles of bubbly.

There are plenty of activities to keep most men happy. A paint-balling day can be great fun (and reasonably cheap) or how about the chance to drive a racing car, or army tank?

On the day

Whatever you do, choose your attendants carefully so you can relax and leave all the tasks up to them.

You were born
together and together
you shall be for ever
more … but let there
be spaces in your
togetherness, and let
the winds of heaven
dance between you.

Kahlil Gibran

Dressed to impress

chapter 7
Dressed to impress

Something old, something new, something borrowed, something blue ...

Something old refers to old friends, and something new your new life together. Something borrowed was traditionally a gift given to the bride by her family for luck, but which had to be returned, and blue is supposed to be the colour of fidelity.

THE BRIDE

No need to rush!

Like all other clothes, fashions in wedding gowns change, so if you're planning a wedding two years' ahead don't be in too much of a hurry to buy your gown. Yes, it's exciting to go trying them on, but you can change your mind several times in the course of a year. You don't want to spend hundreds of pounds only to find something you prefer several months later.

Where?

Where you choose might well depend on your budget. If buying new, the first choice to look will probably be a specialist bridal shop, either independently owned, or part of a franchised chain. Department stores might well have a bridal department within the store and many high street chain stores now have bridal ranges.

A specialist shop will have a range of dresses for you to look at, and often catalogues to order from. Many ask you to make an appointment before arriving. This is an excellent idea as it means you will have the undivided attention of a specialist advisor throughout your visit. Changing rooms tend to be spacious with plenty of room in the shop to walk around to see how the gown feels.

Chain stores will usually be the cheapest option, but the likelihood is that they will have a very limited number of styles. You will probably not have a specialist advisor, and you might not have the comfort of a large changing room.

You can also buy second hand, hire a dress, or have one made. Don't discount charity shops. Some charities have special bridal stores where, as well as donated dresses, they receive new but end-of-line dresses from bridal companies. You could pick up a real designer gown at a bargain price.

When?

Some gowns can be bought straight from stock, but you will have far more choice of style, colour, and price range if you have time to order. Most gowns from specialist bridal shops take five to six months to arrive.

You will need to allow time for fittings. There will usually be one when the gown arrives in the shop to check everything is correct, another for alteration purposes and a final fitting when the dress is collected. The first two might well be done together, and there has to be time for the seamstresses to complete any alterations necessary.

Two's company

When you go to try on dresses take someone with you who you trust to tell you the truth. Another opinion will be extremely useful. However, don't take too many people. They will all have different views and might confuse you or leave you feeling flustered, trying to please everyone. You might think that you have to take all your bridesmaids at the same time, but this can also confuse things. Try to choose their dresses on a day when you don't need to think of your own as well.

Quick tip

DON'T SPOIL THINGS
When going to any shop to try on a wedding gown, avoid wearing any fake tan or other make-up that might rub off. You will not be popular if you leave stains on an expensive dress.

What style?

Be open minded when you go to look for your dream gown. You might have fallen in love with a gown in a bridal magazine but just because it looks great on the model doesn't mean it will look great on you. Dresses in magazines might look beautiful but they have been laid out for the photograph, and pinned and tucked to form the perfect shape.

Take advice from the salesperson. They are experts after all, and don't want you to look awful on your special day.

Make sure you have plenty of time and try on as many as you like. You will know your dress as soon as you try it on!

Quick tip

TROPICAL DREAMS

If you have decided to get married abroad, think carefully about your dress. Wedding gowns can be very heavy to wear because of the various underskirts, beading, and boned bodices. You might want to choose a gown in a lightweight fabric that will be more comfortable to wear in a hot climate.

A reputable bridal retailer will be able to pack your dress ready for you to take abroad with you. If this is not possible, you will need to fold it loosely with layers of acid-free tissue paper, and make sure it is hung up as soon as possible when you reach your destination.

Tattoos

Tattoos are fashionable at the time of writing but will they be when you are 50? You might not want the leaping tiger on your bosom displayed to your grandchildren, so it makes sense to choose a gown that covers it. If you regret a tattoo on your arm, a flimsy stole or pashmina will hide it nicely without spoiling your photos. (See also a tip in the Looking Good section.)

Made to measure

There are designers who will make a gown to your personal requirements, designing a one-off, just for you. This will give you the dress of your dreams, but it comes at a price.

You might have a friend or relative who is handy with the needle and might offer to make your dress for you. This can save you money, but always look at something that she has made. Making a wedding gown is totally different from running up some curtains, especially if you have chosen a delicate fabric or a style that requires boning in the bodice.

Pre-owned

Your local paper will always have a selection of second hand dresses for sale, often at bargain prices. Some of these might never have been worn. Don't feel that they will be unlucky, or that wedding has been called off — it might well be that the bride has put on (or lost) weight, or has changed her mind about style.

If you go to see a pre-owned dress, don't be afraid to ask to try it on. Check, too, to make sure it has been dry-cleaned.

Underpinning

Dresses from specialist bridal shops will usually have been selected from couture ranges and therefore be made with built-in support, avoiding the need for a bra. Cheaper dresses might not have the built-in support.

If you need some sort of support, do get measured at a good lingerie shop. This is especially important when choosing a strapless dress. If necessary take your dress with you so that you can make sure there are no straps showing to spoil your look.

Veils

Try veils on with your gown before buying. Some gowns look better with a short veil, but some require a full length one. Always take advice on the best way to wear one and practise pinning it in before the big day.

Quick tip

GOOSE-BUMPS

If you are planning a winter wedding but still want a glamorous strapless dress, you don't want to appear with goose-pimples in your photos. So it's worth checking if a local gown shop will hire out a velvet cape. These come in a variety of colours and can look really dramatic – and keep a bride warm in between photo shots.

Jewels

Of course, the most important items of jewellery will be the rings. Many jewellers offer discounts on weddings rings when you buy an engagement ring. Some will also offer discounts if you buy a man's and woman's ring at the same time.

Perfect match?

It is a romantic thing to do but don't always think that you have to have matching rings. Not all rings suit all hands and you might need to try several on before you are both happy with the choice.

Allow time for the rings to be altered if the store doesn't have your size in stock. You might also want to have the rings engraved with initials or date. Again, allow time for this to be done.

On the day

Your choice of jewellery will depend on your dress. If you have gone for one with lots of embroidery and beading, it is better to keep your jewellery simple. A plain dress can take much more elaborate jewellery.

If you have a piece of wedding jewellery that has been worn in your family for generations, check well in advance if it needs mending or cleaning. Silver jewellery especially can tarnish if left but can be cleaned very easily.

Don't forget to move your engagement ring to your right hand so that you don't have to remove it to get your wedding ring on.

Shoes

Choose shoes that are going to be comfortable all day – you will be on your feet for several hours. Tight shoes show on your face and you don't want that to happen in your photos.

Practice makes perfect

Practise walking in your dress, especially if you have a long train. You don't want to catch your heel in the train or trip over on your big day.

BRIDESMAIDS

Who chooses?

It is YOUR wedding so choose the colour scheme you want. Remember the first rule of wedding planning – you will always offend someone. However, if you are asking your bridesmaids (or their parents in the case of children) to pay for their dresses, it is polite to discuss colour and style with them first.

If you have set a budget for your bridesmaids' dresses, you will need to divide that amount by the number of attendants to see what you can afford.

Adults

This includes that awkward age between 11 and 16 as well as 'grown-ups'.

Don't be afraid to use a bit of imagination. You don't have to go to a bridal shop these days. Some high street stores sell bridal wear, including good ranges of bridesmaids' dresses, although the choice of colour will almost certainly be limited.

Do you want outfits that your bridesmaids can wear again? There must be loads of unworn satin numbers at the backs of wardrobes. So try shops that sell evening wear. Many have ranges of gowns that can be used as bridesmaids' dresses. There are also many shops that hire prom dresses, another good place to look. Separates are also a good bet. Corset tops can be worn out clubbing with jeans afterwards!

Little girls grow up

Little bridesmaids grow very quickly and unless they've got a party coming up, the chances are that they will never wear their dresses again. So why pay the earth for them? Chain stores, and even some supermarkets, sell ranges of bridesmaids' dresses. They'll probably be cream or white but add a silk ribbon sash and stitch some small silk flowers in your colour scheme over the skirt. Designer dresses – at a fraction of designer prices!

Style?

Mini versions of the adult bridesmaids' dresses won't always suit a little girl. It's better to choose a colour to match rather than a style.

Choose a style that is practical and comfortable for them to wear. As with the bride, non-slip shoes are a must! Head-dresses, too, should be light and comfortable so that they don't get taken off before the ceremony. Little children will almost certainly start to run around and play later in the day so be prepared for them to become untidy.

Let little girls practise walking in their dresses and new shoes.

Brrrrrrrrr. . .

Adrenalin can keep a bride warm, even on the coldest of days, but what about the bridesmaids? Even in the middle of summer, little ones can get very cold standing around while photos are being taken, so don't condemn them to being wrapped in anoraks that someone fishes from a car. You can get woollen shrugs or cardis especially for bridesmaids, which will keep them warm and still look pretty.

THE MEN FOLK

Most men will say they don't like the fuss of dressing up but will almost certainly make the effort for The Day. It is usual, but not compulsory, to have the groom, best man, ushers, and fathers in the same style clothes. For a small wedding, you can save money by asking the men to wear their own suits, possibly all having the same ties to match the general colour scheme.

Morning dress

It is rare these days for men to own a morning suit so hiring is the obvious solution. If using an independent local shop, you will need to book the suits fairly early on as they might not have enough stock for more than one wedding in a day. The shops owned by a chain will have more flexibility.

Most chains will offer a selection of suit styles and colour schemes. Many couples will choose to have all the men in the same style suit with waistcoats and cravats in the general colour scheme. However, the groom can choose to have something slightly different, e.g. a velvet or brocade jacket, to make him stand out from the rest of the men.

When the suits are delivered, always check to see that they are the right size, especially the shirt collar sizes, and that the waistcoats are all the same. It is not unheard-of for six suits to be delivered all with different waistcoat materials. If this happens, ring up straight away and request that they be changed.

Kilts

Families with Scottish (or Cornish or Welsh) connections often opt for the men to wear the kilt. Again, these are available to hire and usually come as a full set with choice of jacket, sporran, etc. You can have great fun researching the family tartan!

Little boys

It is a fact of life that little boys would much prefer to be wearing jeans than a fancy suit. If velvet knee breeches are your dream, the chances are that only very young, or very well-bribed, boys will wear them willingly. However, there are plenty of options.

Morning dress for young boys can be hired to match the male adults. Kilts too can be hired in very small sizes. Some hire shops will also stock miniature versions of military uniforms—ideal if you are having a military wedding—and boys will almost certainly enjoy the thought of dressing as a soldier or sailor.

A simple option is to have the youngsters wearing plain long trousers and a shirt, with a waistcoat to match your colour scheme. This looks smart, is easy to wear, and the waistcoats can be taken off after the photos have been taken.

Taking back

If you are hiring clothes, make sure someone reliable is in charge of taking them back. You are likely to have gone on your honeymoon and don't want to get back to irate phone calls because the suits have not been returned. Always empty the pockets before the suits are returned to the store.

Mum!

It is a good idea for both mothers to check what each is wearing before the Big Day. While two guests can get away with wearing the same outfits, the same can't be said for the important mothers.

Some mothers decide to go for the same colour as the bridesmaids to keep in with the bride's colour scheme. This can look very pretty but runs the risk of the bride's mother merging into the background in the photos.

Quick tip

HATS OR NO HATS?
Hats are traditional for weddings but many women are nervous about wearing them. Some brides specify if they wish their guests to wear hats but this can add to the expense for some people. It is usually best left to individuals to choose. However, it is usual for both mothers to do the same as each other, i.e. both wearing hats or neither.

Themed weddings

Themed weddings can be great fun especially for people who enjoy dressing up. There are, though, a few pitfalls to consider.

It is important that everyone joins in the fun of a theme. Some people might dread the thought of dressing up and could spoil the day if they arrive in traditional wedding outfits.

You might dream of floating down the aisle in a mediaeval gown but will the men folk be as happy to wear tights? Unless you have a particular period in mind, try to choose something that everyone will be comfortable with.

If you have decided on a theme, let your guests know well in advance so that they have time to hire or make costumes.

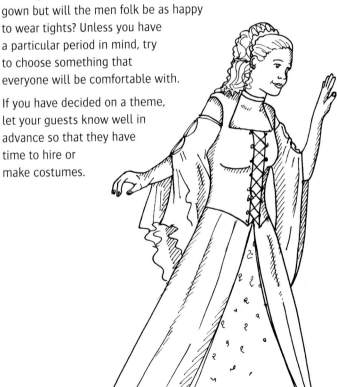

Though it rains,
I won't get wet;
I'll use your love
for an umbrella.

Japanese folk song

Looking good

chapter 8
Looking good

Appointments

If you are going to a hair or beauty salon, book your appointment well in advance. On popular wedding days in the summer, the early appointments can be booked months in advance. If your wedding is before lunch, you will need to be at the salon early.

Don't forget that your bridesmaids and mother will also need hair and beauty appointments. If you are all going to the same salon, ask if they take block bookings.

Order?

You should have your hair done before any make-up. If you put your make-up on first, it will almost certainly wash off when the hairdresser starts to do your hair.

If your hair and beauty appointments are at different salons, make the appointments to allow plenty of time to get from one to the other.

Some salons will allow a stylist or beautician to go to your home on the day of the wedding. This makes sense but will almost certainly cost you more as you will have to make up for the time lost in the salon. You might also have to pay taxi fares. As with the salon appointments, make sure you allow plenty of time for the hairdresser to finish her work before the beautician starts on your make-up.

Where?

You might be going back to your home town to get married so need to find a local hairdresser or beautician. Do this well before the wedding. If necessary, make a special trip for this alone. Ask around for personal recommendations if you haven't lived there for a while and have lost track of your old salons. You might end up having three hair dos in one day but that won't matter if you get the right person in the end.

There are now many mobile hair stylists and beauticians offering hair and beauty appointments in your home, with special offers for weddings. These can be a really good idea but, again, always have a trial run first.

The practice run

If you are having your hair and/or make-up done by a professional, always have at least one practice run before the special day. This is especially vital if you have long hair and are having it put up for the occasion.

Don't spoil things

Whatever happens, don't wear something to the hairdresser that needs to be pulled over your head to remove. Wear a buttoned shirt or a little camisole that won't destroy your hairdresser's work of art. Arrange to be picked up outside the salon. It is very embarrassing to walk through town to a car park in your jeans.... with a tiara and veil!

If you've got long hair and are having it put up, you might need to wash it the evening before. Fine hair can be very flyaway if freshly washed, and impossible to style as you want it.

BITS & PIECES

Hair ornaments on combs can slip out very easily. It is a better idea to use clips to fasten flowers etc. into your hair.

Keep it natural

Don't try anything too extreme with your wedding make-up. Natural looks best.

If you are going to have your make-up done by a professional, always have at least one trial. Their idea of colours might not be yours, and you don't want to be stuck with something you don't like on The Day.

A trial should take about an hour and once you are both satisfied with the result, the make-up on the day should take about 30 minutes.

Making it last

Weddings always involve loads of kissing. To make your lipstick last, first use a natural concealer over your lips. Then apply two coats of lipstick, blotting the first with a tissue before putting the second on. Lastly, apply either a coat of gloss, or— a beautician's tip—translucent powder. Your lippie should last for ages!

However, pop your lipstick into your little bag of essentials, ready to top up before the reception.

Tears!

Weddings can also be tearful occasions and you don't want to look like a clown with black marks running down your face. Always choose waterproof mascara and test it first to make sure it doesn't run. Mums will also find this tip useful – they are the ones who tend to cry the most!

Quick tip

SPOTS!

If a zit erupts the day before the wedding, try dabbing on some lavender oil or some toothpaste. This will dry the spot and take away the redness. If one appears on the actual day, don't panic. Use a concealer stick under your foundation and no-one will know it was even there.

A golden glow

If you are planning to have an instant tan, always have a trial session first to check the colour.

Have an instant tan about two days before the wedding. This will give the colour time to develop properly. It should last about a week, so if you are planning an exotic honeymoon, you will still be able to arrive with a golden glow, ready to hit the beach.

To make the tan last, keep your skin moisturised. However, dips in the sea or the pool will make it fade quicker.

Don't mistake an instant tan for the real thing. It won't protect you against the sun's rays!

"We are all a bit weird and life's a little weird, and when we find someone whose weirdness is compatible with ours, we join up with them and fall in mutual weirdness and call it love."

Anon

Mind the strap marks!

If you have chosen a strapless dress, don't be tempted to go sunbathing just before your wedding. Red sunburn is not flattering, and white strap marks can completely spoil the look of your dress. An instant tan will disguise strap marks slightly but not fully.

Quick tip

WINTER WHITE

If you're having a winter wedding but plan on wearing a strapless or low-backed gown, don't forget your back. It will be on show and you don't want the camera to catch the spots that tend to accumulate under winter sweaters.

An exfoliating back scrub will help but, even better, is to treat yourself to a shoulders and back treatment at a beauty salon or spa. If you have lots of spots, a sunbed will help to dry them up, but these are not recommended for constant use because of the dangers to skin.

Tattoos

It might be worth consulting an expert as you can obtain specialist cover products that claim to cover tattoos and other skin blemishes. If using them yourself it is best to practise several times with these products as skin colour must be matched exactly and might take mixes of various shades.

Waxing

Have legs (and anywhere else) waxed at least two days before
your wedding, in case you get those nasty red spots. This should
give them time to fade but your skin will still be hair-free.

Emergency supplies

You don't want to be topping up make-up etc. all day but
a few necessities can be put into a little dolly bag to match
your dress. Or you can get Mum to keep them in her handbag.
Lipstick will almost certainly be needed after all the kissing,
and a hair brush, especially if you've travelled by an open car or
horse and carriage. Your foundation should last all day, but you
might want some powder to dab on if your nose gets shiny.

For him

It's not just the bride who wants to look good on the wedding
day. The groom should have his hair cut a few days beforehand
to avoid that 'just cut' look. It's probably not a good idea to
try a new hair style specially for the wedding so, if you fancy
a change, have a practice run several weeks beforehand so that
it has time to grow out if you don't like it.

Designer stubble can look scruffy with a morning suit. Why not
treat yourself to the full works at a traditional barber and have
a proper shave?

The groom's hands will also be on show, especially if he is
wearing a wedding ring. If you have a manual job, or love
tinkering with car engines, try to get rid of all the oil stains etc.
before the day.

BEATING THE BUTTERFLIES

Last minute nerves

Hers

There's not a bride on earth who hasn't suffered from nerves on her wedding day. If you let them, they can spoil your day but there are several easy ways of overcoming your nerves. Read the section on choosing your attendants. This is where it will pay dividends to have someone who is calm and doing her job.

Even if you don't usually eat breakfast, find time to have a snack some time during the preparations. Trips to the hairdresser and having make-up done all take time and it's easy to forget that you haven't eaten. You don't want to feel faint because of lack of food.

Space

Try not to have too many people to your house before the ceremony. Obviously your close family will be there, plus your bridesmaids, but don't encourage the rest of your family to turn up for snacks and wine. You might love them all dearly but you can have too much fussing. If they insist, tell them you want your appearance to be a surprise – it usually works!

Allow a few minutes to yourself before leaving for the ceremony. Enjoy that last minute glass of wine or cigarette if it helps to calm the nerves, but remember to spray some breath freshener afterwards.

Rescue

Take a bottle of Bach Rescue Remedy in the car with you. This is an herbal remedy that you can get from health shops and chemists. A few drops on your tongue work wonders.

His

The groom might well feel fine all morning – after all, it's not manly to admit to nerves. However, most grooms will suddenly get butterflies either just before leaving for the church, or just as they arrive. Have a good breakfast (or lunch if the wedding is in the afternoon). You don't want to pass out in the middle of the ceremony.

Now is the time you will appreciate choosing a reliable best man. One calming drink is OK but more than that is likely to make things worse. So the best man shouldn't encourage you to drink more than one. If you have a drink or a cigarette, remember to use a quick spray of breath freshener.

Both of you

Superstition says that the groom shouldn't see the bride before the ceremony. But that doesn't apply to the phone. A quick call or text might be all that's needed to keep the nerves at bay.

Relax!

When you get to the entrance, stand still for a couple of moments and take some deep breaths. Remember what is important. You are going to marry the person you love. The rest of the people around are your friends and family come to help you celebrate. Enjoy yourselves!

Marriage is like
a box of chocolates.
You have to squeeze
a few bottoms to
make sure you like
what you are getting.

Anon

Arriving
in style

chapter 9
Arriving in style

Perhaps you ought to walk to church. That way you'll have more chance of seeing some of the lucky symbols associated with weddings. It is supposed to be lucky to see a rainbow, a black cat, or a sweep!

However, walking is normally impractical so …

Who goes in what?

It is the best man's duty to get the groom to the venue on time. These days, this usually involves booking a taxi (making sure it's booked in plenty of time) but if the best man wants to do something original he can hire a Ferrari, a fire engine, or even a helicopter.

Generally, the bridesmaids and bride's mother travel to the venue together, a few minutes before the bride and her escort.

What to choose

There is a vast range of vehicles and other ways of getting to the church on time but you need to be a bit realistic and find out what's available in your area. If you want something different that has to come from another part of the county, you will have to pay a premium – not just for the mileage, but for the extra time that vehicle is away from home.

Spare a thought for the horse

Before you book a horse and carriage, check the distance they
will cover. Some companies will only allow their horses to pull
a carriage for a couple of miles. If your dream is to drive off
from the venue in a carriage, but the reception is a long way
off, you might have to change to a car on the way. If you live in
a hilly area, you might also find it difficult to book a carriage.

CARS

Something borrowed

You might be lucky enough to have a relative or friend with
a super car, who offers you the use of it on the day – possibly
as a wedding present. This is great and will save you money, but
it is worth checking that the owner has the proper insurance for
the vehicle.

Also make sure you can rely on the owner to turn up on time
with both the car and himself in immaculate condition – you
don't want to have to visit the car wash on the way.

Take a look

There is a vast choice of cars around, and a huge variety in costs. Always go to see the cars before booking (or send a reliable person if you are trying to book your wedding at a distance). A vehicle that looks great in a photo or on a website might really be rusty or have bumps in places that show.

Make sure that you know what the model of car looks like. Many brides have been disappointed to find a modern Rolls Royce arriving at her door, when she's been expecting a vintage one.

Don't be afraid to ask to see photos with the chauffeur in. You want someone who is going to turn up looking smart on the day, not someone in shorts and a T-shirt! And don't be afraid to ask if you can see the cars at an actual wedding. This will give you a good idea of their turn-out and how helpful the chauffeurs are.

A good chauffeur will help you in and out of the car, making sure that your dress or veil doesn't get caught. He will also take charge of your bouquet so that it doesn't get crushed. He should also be proficient with an umbrella so that you don't get wet if it is raining.

The open road

There can be nothing more dramatic than driving off from your wedding in an open car but make sure there is a water-tight hood in case the weather is bad. Open cars can be very draughty so it would be a good idea to travel to the venue with the hood up so that you don't get windswept before arriving for the ceremony.

How long?

When booking cars, always check how long the cars are available for. A church wedding usually takes around 40-45 minutes, with about the same for photos afterwards.

A reputable company will normally say that you have got the cars for as long as the wedding takes (usually 3 hours to allow for travel time) but some will quote for the minimum time, e.g. 1½ hours, and charge extra for any time over that.

Some wedding ceremonies take longer than the average 45 minutes. As an example, a Nuptial Mass or a wedding with a musical concert can take up to twice as long. If you are planning a longer ceremony, always have the courtesy to discuss this with the car company.

If you want to go to a second venue for photos, always check if the company is willing to do so and if there is an extra charge. The cars might have been booked for a second wedding later than yours and it can be very embarrassing if the chauffeur refuses to take you to the second venue because you haven't mentioned it and booked the extra time.

If your wedding is a civil one at a hotel, ask if the cars can wait till after the ceremony so that you can have photos taken with them.

How many cars?

You will need one vehicle for the bride to travel to the venue with her escort. If you have bridesmaids, they have to get there as well, so many couples book two cars. However, if you live near the venue, a company might be prepared to make two trips; the first with the bridesmaids and bride's mother, then returning for the bride. If you choose to do this, always make sure there is time to do the return journey, especially if your wedding is in a busy area of town.

Unless you are having a wedding and reception in the same place, remember that the bridesmaids have to get to the reception after the ceremony. Very little children might prefer to go with their parents and calm down after all the excitement and photos. If you have only used one car for the journey to the venue, it is unlikely that you can do the same after the ceremony. The bridesmaids would be left on their own waiting for the car to come back.

Some couples like to provide a special car for the groom's parents or for grandparents. This is a nice touch but not essential. Again, you might find that your chosen company will do an extra journey, but always ask well before the day and be prepared for an extra charge.

If you decide to use cars from two different companies, it is courtesy to tell each of them. Most companies will work happily together but they need to know which car is carrying out which task, and they might need to liaise on times.

Try for size

When you go to view a choice of cars, don't be afraid to ask if you can sit in one. You have to be sure that you can get in and out of the car gracefully so imagine that you are wearing a full gown, not jeans. Make sure the door is big enough and that you don't have to clamber over a front seat (sometimes the case with vintage cars).

Don't forget Dad!

It is important that you choose cars that are big enough for the number of people. If you have several bridesmaids, you need to tell your car company so that they can recommend a vehicle. There are very few modern cars that will take over five passengers, so you might need a limousine. Again, check your numbers with the company as there are strict regulations for the number of passengers allowed to be carried.

When you leave the ceremony, there will be one extra person to travel with the bridesmaids – the bride's escort. He (or she) is often forgotten when calculating numbers.

Quick tip

DECORATIONS
It is traditional to have ribbons on a bridal car (or horse and carriage) and almost certainly these will be provided. If you want a colour other than white or ivory, you will need to discuss this beforehand to check that it is possible. There are some colours that are almost impossible to find in ribbons but most requests can be accommodated.

Bubbly

If your fantasy is driving off toasting each other with a glass of bubbly, check with the car company. Some companies will provide this as a matter of course, but there are strict licensing laws in some parts of the country and they might not be allowed to provide this service. There should, however, be no objection to you providing your own bottle.

Weather or not . . .

Ask if umbrellas are carried in the cars. If not, you will have to make sure someone is on hand with one if it happens to rain.

Transport for your guests

Although most people these days have their own cars, many would prefer not to use them because of the drink/drive laws. It can make sense to hire a bus to transport your guests from the wedding venue to the reception (if the Royal Family can do it, why not everyone else?).

If guests are staying at hotels, it can be a good idea to hire the bus for the whole day and have them all collected. This can work out cheaper than booking taxis. If you do this, nominate one of the guests as the conductor, giving him a list of all the people to be collected and the venues. This way, you will ensure that no-one has been forgotten.

You will need to stress to your guests the importance of catching the bus on time. Just a couple of minutes waiting for an aunt to find her hat or shoes in one hotel, followed by a few more while uncle finishes a drink in another, can make your guests very late for the ceremony.

Finding the way

If your guests do not know the area, put a map in with the wedding invitation, or directions from their hotel to the venue. This is especially important if there are several churches with the same name; it is amazing how many St. Mary's can be found in one town!

I add my breath
   to your breath
That our days may
   be long in the earth
That the days of our
   people may be long
That we may be one
   person
That we may finish
   our roads together.

Keres Indian Song

Flash, bang, wallop

chapter 10
Flash, bang, wallop!

You will almost certainly find that your wedding day simply flies by. So you need to capture the day, either in photos or on video (or both) so that you can look back at it and remember all the little details.

Remember that your day should be a 'Once Only' day and you won't be able to repeat the photographs.

Most of these tips apply to both photographers and videographers.

Who to choose

The old saying "You get what you pay for" is never truer than when it comes to choosing a photographer or videographer. Prices and quality vary enormously, so ask around for personal recommendations (or complaints).

Even if you've had a personal recommendation always ask to see the photographer's portfolios or a finished DVD. If you've got time, try to see the photographer at work at a wedding. This will give you a good idea of his/her style and approach.

If you are having both still and video, it is a courtesy to inform each one. Most local companies will be used to working with each other but it is worth checking to see if they are both happy. You might find that they contact each other before the wedding to check on locations etc.

Insurance

There are several professional organisations that your photographer might belong to. These are a good indication of the quality of his/her work but they do not offer any guarantees or insurance against shoddy work. Always ask if your photographer has got Public Liability and Public Indemnity Insurance. This should cover you against any mishaps caused by him/her on the day. But also, don't forget your own vital wedding insurance which should insure you against failure of your precious photos or film.

Personal touch

The most important thing when it comes to choosing a photographer is that you are comfortable with him or her. Many people don't realise just how much the photographer takes over your day. From the time you arrive at the venue (and possibly even before that, at your house) the photographer will be there with you, recording every move you make. If you've booked someone you've taken a dislike to, it can completely spoil your special day.

Always ask to meet the person who will be taking your photographs. You might be very comfortable with the person who has taken your booking but some photography companies employ several associates who only attend on the day and might never have seen you before. It can be quite a shock to find a complete stranger taking over your wedding!

Chains

You might be tempted by a special deal from a chain of photographers. These can often be very good offers but there are a couple of things to check.

The rep who comes to your house will have a variety of samples. He is unlikely to tell you that they are by different people. Most will be part-time photographers. This does not mean that they are bad at their job but might be less skilled at organisation. If the company is unwilling to show you samples of a specific person's work, it might well be worth reconsidering before you part with any deposit.

Make sure that the photographer will be from the local area. This might sound obvious but some chains will send the nearest available photographer who might live some distance away. This means that he/she might not have been to the venue before, or had time to study it for the best settings. Check also that you know who the photographer is and that you have a personal contact number for him so that if, by any horrible chance, he is not at the venue, you can contact him to see what is happening.

Friend or family

If you have an offer of photography by a friend who is a very good photographer, the same rules apply. Make sure he/she is familiar with the venue; if they live away from the area, ask them to make a special trip before the wedding so that you can be confident that they know where to get the best shots. Don't be afraid to turn down their offer if you feel that they haven't got the personality to control the guests.

How much?

There are huge differences in the way that photographers price their services. This can make it difficult to compare prices. Don't be afraid to ask exactly what you are getting for your money. Some photographers will give a special deal for Register Office weddings, or for mid-week occasions.

Check out:

Ask if the cost includes photos taken at the reception. Many photographers will include the ceremony and reception (up to the first dance) in the costs; others will charge you by the hour. You should always make sure you know what's included before you book.

Check if the price includes photos taken at the bride's house before the wedding. If you want to have photos at the house, ask if the photographer has an assistant – or if he/she works with a partner. Most photographers like to be at the church to take photos of the guests arriving, and especially of the groom and his best man who should be at the church at least 30 minutes before the ceremony is due to start.

If there is only one person doing the whole lot of photos, it will be quite a rush to get from the bride's house to the church in time. Also, if you (the bride) live quite a distance away, it means you might have to be dressed in your finery at least an hour before you are due to leave for the church.

If there are two photographers, this makes life a lot easier.

How many?

The number of photos varies considerably. The ideal is for there to be unlimited shots. However, some photographers will limit you to a certain number, especially with their budget package; 36 might sound like a lot but these can be used up very quickly and some less scrupulous photographers will then demand more money to take further photos. It is not easy to refuse on the day!

Always ask how many prints will be included in the final package and how much extra ones will cost. Again, this varies greatly and will, to a certain extent, depend on the number of photos taken. However, most packages will offer a set number with the opportunity to buy more. Many photographers now offer a range of sizes so that you can make up a modern album with a variety of sizes on each page.

Quick tip

GIVING AWAY

Don't forget that extra photos can increase the final bill considerably so don't start promising everyone a copy. After the wedding, you can always show your guests the wedding photos and give them a price list so that they can order their own if they wish.

Album?

Most photographers will offer a range of albums at an extra price but generally it is not compulsory to buy one from him.

Formal or informal?

Most photographers will use the terms Formal and Informal to describe the style of photos. Formal shots are those which are posed and organised by the photographer. You will be aware that the photos are being taken.

Informal shots are those where you haven't been asked to pose in any way. Images will be taken as they happen. Most people hate having their photos taken, so shots taken when you're not posing are often the best.

Another term you might hear is reportage photography. This, again, is an informal approach where your wedding will be captured in a photojournalist way – capturing everything as it happens. It is also sometimes called documentary wedding photography where the photographer does not intrude or ask guests to pose.

It is vital that you discuss the style of photography that you want. Most couples these days tend to shy away from the posed shots of yesteryear but go for a more informal approach with just a few formal photos. If a photographer works with a partner, you will often find that one takes the formal shots, while the other is capturing different angles and perspectives.

Quick tip

A WORD OF WARNING
If you decide to go for all informal shots, be prepared for a few moans. Gran will have paid out for a new outfit and will expect to have a photo with you to show it off!

Schedule

If you are having some posed shots, you need to decide on which ones before the actual day, and make sure that your photographer has the full details. There can be nothing worse than a photographer who continually asks you what shots you would like him to do.

Most will have a general schedule to suggest to you but there are always variations in family relationships and you want to keep embarrassing situations to a minimum. Your photos won't be very pleasant if Aunty Jane and Aunty Vera, who haven't spoken to each other for years, are asked to stand next to one another and smile.

Try to arrange to meet your photographer about two weeks before the day. That way, you can go over any last minute changes to your list. It is also helpful for the photographer to remind him/herself about what you look like. He might not have seen you for two years and your appearance might give him some ideas about suitable shots and poses.

On the day

The quicker the formal shots are done, the better they are likely to be. Most people get bored having to stand around waiting to be called and no-one wants photos where all the guests are looking fed-up. This is where the schedule proves to be extremely useful.

Trust the expert

If you have chosen your photographer because you love the work he's produced, trust him on the day. Don't assume that the best shots will be taken in bright sunlight. If he suggests a shady area, go with it. It will be a lot more flattering with no squinting or facial shadows.

Second venue

Photographers will often suggest a second venue for photos. They usually have favourite places, such as parks or gardens, where they know that romantic photos can be taken. Also you might have a favourite romantic spot where you would like to have some photos taken. Usually, only the bride and groom go, but some couples choose to take their attendants.

If the venue is the photographer's choice, he will check that he has permission to go there. However, if it is your own choice, you will need to make sure that it is OK to be there and that there is access for the wedding car.

If the photographer suggests a second venue, make sure that it is included in the original price quote. It is not unheard of for the service to be added on later as an extra.

Moving image

A wedding video (these days usually a DVD) can be a lasting memory of your special day. Many people these days have their own video cameras and someone will almost certainly offer to do the filming for you. However, unless the friend or relative is an expert with professional editing equipment, the finished article is likely to be less than perfect.

How long?

The average wedding video will last around **90** minutes and, properly edited, will cover all aspects of your day. You will need to discuss your requirements with the videographers but, generally speaking, they will start filming about an hour before the wedding and go up until the first dance at the reception.

Musical accompaniment

Most companies will use music as a background to the film. However, you need to be aware that you might not be able to choose your own. Music is copyrighted and can only be used if a licence has been paid for.

Professional editing equipment will allow the sound of the bells (often very loud and overpowering on amateur videos) to be faded into the background.

Take a look

As with the photographer, it is helpful to see a videographer at work. Some might object to being inspected but you can usually watch a wedding as a casual onlooker if you know where he is going to be working.

You don't want a camera in your face throughout the day recording every word you say. The best films will be those where the couple and guests are hardly aware that they are being filmed.

If the videographer looks relaxed, then so will you!

Smile!

Two souls but with a single thought. Two hearts that beat as one.

Friedrich Halm

Flower power

chapter 11
Flower power

When you choose your bouquet, look at the meanings of the flowers.

Roses have always been a symbol of Love, but Orange Blossom has also been traditionally used for bouquets as it symbolises Purity and Loveliness. Carnations denote Devoted Love and Orchids mean Beauty. What more could any bride ask for on her wedding day?

Who's going to do your flowers?

Unless you have seen their finished work, be very careful if a friend or neighbour offers to do your flowers. Making a wedding bouquet is a specialised art. Just because someone can make a pretty flower arrangement, it does not follow that they can produce a bouquet that will survive the knocks of your wedding day without falling apart.

You will need to book your florist fairly early on in the proceedings. Many florists will only commit to doing a maximum of two weddings on a particular day and the better ones get booked up very quickly.

You will need to meet with your florist about six to eight weeks before the wedding to finalise your requirements.

AT THE FLORIST

Always ask if you can see a finished bouquet before booking a florist. Flowers that have been simply pushed into a foam holder will just as simply fall out. Many brides have arrived at the church in tears because their bouquets have fallen to pieces in the car. A bouquet can take some knocks so check that the florist wires the flowers or fastens them securely.

Which to choose

Discuss your requirements carefully. Most flowers are now available throughout the year, the exception being spring flowers. A good florist will be able to advise you on your choice.

It's a good idea to cut out pictures from magazines when you see a bouquet you like. This makes it much easier than trying to describe the shape you want.

Take in swatches of material, or a ribbon, in your chosen colour. Again this makes it easier for the florist to choose flowers of the exact colour.

Children

Check the size of the bridesmaids' bouquets carefully. Flowers can be very heavy, especially if they are wired. Little hands can find carrying a large bouquet very difficult so ask for smaller ones if possible.

Another option is to give your little attendants a small basket of flowers or a teddy bear to carry — these can be dressed to match your colour scheme. Be careful though, if you are tempted by the idea of a wand. Pretty—yes—but ideal for hitting other attendants over the head with!

Buttonholes

It is usual to provide a corsage for both mothers and buttonholes for the main male participants i.e. groom, best man, ushers and fathers. Some couples like to provide buttonholes for all the guests but this is not obligatory and can add a lot of expense. It is a nice touch, though, to provide a pretty corsage for grandmothers.

You can have your own choice of flowers for the buttonholes but usually men prefer something fairly simple, although superstition says that it should be the same as one from the bride's bouquet. Large ivy leaves behind the flower can look like a bat flying across a jacket!

Although you might want everyone to have the same colours, it might be diplomatic to ask the mothers what colour they are wearing. Your choice of colour might look awful on the mother-in-law's outfit.

The men wear their buttonholes on the left lapel and ladies on the right.

Most florists will provide pins to fasten the buttonholes. However, these can leave marks on fine fabrics and it can be awkward to attach the flowers at the right angle. You can get magnetic buttons — one is attached to the flower, the other goes behind the fabric. These are ideal but might not work properly on thicker fabrics.

Romantic Valentine

It is so romantic to want red roses at a St. Valentine's Day wedding, but check that your florist is willing to do a bouquet for you – and how much she will charge. Florists can make big profits on single red roses on that day, and are also very busy. Some are unwilling to use their supply in a bouquet, or will charge a great deal extra.

Keeping fresh

Most reputable florists will deliver your flowers on the morning of the wedding. If your wedding is late afternoon, tell the florist. With luck they will agree to deliver nearer the time so that your flowers are kept in their cool storage for as long as possible.

If you have to keep your flowers at home for any length of time, put them in a cool place. Sometimes they come packaged in water; leave them in the packaging until you are ready to use them ... but make sure there are no drops of water ready to spill onto your gown.

Quick tip

OTHER FLOWERS

You might also want your florist to make table decorations or flowers for inside or outside the church. These can include arches for the outside of the church, or small topiary trees decorated with ribbons to match your colour scheme. If you want to take these off to the reception, make sure you get someone reliable to collect them after the ceremony – and that they've got a big enough car!

Beware!

Oriental Lilies have stamens which shed pollen that stains. A florist will normally remove these before making a bouquet but if a friend is doing the flowers for you, make sure they know to do this. You don't want a bright yellow stain down the front of your gown!

Throwing the bouquet

It might seem like fun to toss your bouquet into the crowd at the church but once you've done that, you've lost it. Even if the catcher hands it back to you, it is liable to be damaged. Remember, there are likely to be other photos at the reception where you will need to carry your flowers. If you really want to carry out this tradition, but you want to keep your bouquet, you could order a little posy of flowers, especially for throwing. Another idea is to toss the bouquet as you leave the reception.

Preserving your bouquet

You can now have your bouquet preserved as a reminder of your special day. At one time, the only way to do this was by pressing the flowers (which can still be carried out). However, there are now firms which will dry the bouquet and mount it in a 3D box frame, so that it looks exactly the same.

If you choose to have this done, your bouquet will need to be kept cool. The firm should arrange to have it collected as soon after your reception as possible, while the flowers are still fresh.

If you decide after the wedding that you would have liked this done, many of the same firms will re-construct your bouquet from clear photos.

There are three
things that last:
faith, hope and love,
and the greatest
of these is love.

1 Corinthians 13, 13

Happy
ever after

chapter 12
Happy ever after

I t was considered unlucky for the bride to trip on her way into her new home so the groom should carry her over the threshold.

The honeymoon

No – definitely no tips on what to do on honeymoon! They can be found in another book! Just a few general points.

Where to go

Traditionally it was the groom's job to book the honeymoon and surprise the bride with the destination. This sounds romantic and certainly can be, but he should at least give the bride an idea about the sort of holiday it is likely to be. No bride wants to arrive with a suitcase full of bikinis and sun lotion to find that they are on a climbing holiday in the Scottish Highlands. This could mean the end to a very short marriage!

Passports

Check that both passports are in date. Remember it can take several weeks to get new ones.

Ladies – some countries will not let you in if you have not amended your passport to your new name, even if you have your marriage certificate with you. You can apply for a changed passport up to three months ahead of the wedding, although you will not be able to use it until you are legally married.

Planning

If you are going to an exotic destination, check if you need vaccinations or tablets well in advance. You don't want to be suffering the after-effects from any nasty jabs on your wedding day. If you take your itinerary to your GP's practice or a Travel Clinic, they will advise if you need anti-malarial tablets. If so, you must remember that, to be effective, the whole course needs to be taken.

In this unsettled world, it is also worth checking the Foreign Office website in case there is advice on travelling to some of the more exotic locations.

Other websites will give unbiased comments on hotels and resorts. These are always worth looking at before booking, especially if it is to be a once-in-a-lifetime holiday costing a lot of money. A honeymoon is not the time to be going for budget deals and second-rate hotels.

Don't leave it till the day of the wedding to get all your tickets etc together. Make a pack of everything you need such as tickets, passports, insurance details and put it somewhere safe where you will remember it!

Bag of tricks

Always leave your cases somewhere extremely secure where your guests cannot get into them. In these days of heightened security, you don't want to be stopped at the airport for having handcuffs etc. in your luggage. Similarly, confetti sprinkled throughout a case takes forever to get out of clothes.

And a big thank you

You're home, the honeymoon's over and it's back to work. The wedding seems like a distant memory but there's one more thing to think about. Saying 'thank you'.

In these days of phone and email technology, letters might seem old-fashioned but they are still considered part of the etiquette of weddings.

Thank you letters don't have to be long and involved but they will certainly be appreciated. You might well have bought pre-printed thank you cards as part of your stationery package but it is always a polite thing to include a personal note and the name of the present to show the sender that you've remembered what it was. (This is where the list from the section on presents comes in handy.)

So, if you've got a pretty card saying *thank you for your present* you can just add in your own handwriting "John and I really loved the clock you gave us".

If you are writing your own letters, a typical thank you might be:

Dear Aunty xxxx,

Thank you so much for the tea-towels you sent us. I'm sure they will be put to good use when John does the washing-up! It is a pity you weren't able to travel to the wedding but I hope you like the photo I have included.

Thank you again.

Love from

Ann

Hi-tech DIY

In these days of computer wizardry, it's relatively simple to produce your own cards with a photo of the wedding. It makes a nice souvenir, especially for people who sent a present but didn't attend the wedding.

Quick tip

LET THEM HAVE CAKE

If invited guests have been unable to attend the wedding, you can send a small piece of wedding cake with your thank you letter. You can buy special boxes to send it in. However, if you had a sponge cake, this might not be such a good idea as it will probably be stale by the time you get back from honeymoon.

Parents

If parents have contributed to the finance or organisational details of the wedding, it is a nice touch to send a card or letter to show your appreciation.

Good service

Many companies who provide services for weddings are relatively small and often run as part-time businesses. Even though you have paid for their product, if you have received good service a little thank you note will be much appreciated. Personal recommendations make good advertising.

CHECK LISTS

ONCE YOU'VE NAMED THE DAY

Decide on the date

Ensure you have the right documents to book wedding

Book venue for ceremony

Decide on the budget

Book venue for reception

Guest list

Choose attendants

Order stationery

Book transport

Choose colour scheme

Book the florist

Gift list

Make a checklist of dates for payments etc.

Send out invitations

Keep list of replies and numbers

CHURCH WEDDING

Discuss Order of Service with minister

Book choir

Book bells

Choose hymns

Ask if photography is allowed

Check if confetti is allowed

CIVIL WEDDING

Produce correct identification documents

Decide on form of service

Choose readings if required

Choose music if required

Book Registrar if getting married in an approved venue

HOTEL RECEPTION

Pay deposit

Choose menu

Choose drinks package

Book toastmaster if required

Give guests menu choices, if necessary

Make small menus for tables as reminders

Table decorations and balloons etc.

Order cake

Favours

Book rooms if people are staying overnight

Seating plan

Write out place cards

Final numbers to venue

Pay balance

DIY RECEPTION

Order marquee if required
Choose menu
Book caterer
Buy food if freezing
Decide who is doing what
Buy or order drinks
Crockery
Glasses
Order or buy cake
Table linen
Table decorations and
  balloons etc.
Seating plan if formal tables
Write out place cards

EVENING RECEPTION

Decide on number of guests
Make guest list and send
  invitations
Choose menu
Book disco
Book other entertainment if
  appropriate

CLOTHES

Choose wedding dress
Book dates for fittings
Choose bridesmaids' dresses
Book mens' outfits if hiring
All men measured for suits

HAIR & BEAUTY

Book hair appointment for
  yourself and bridesmaids
Book make-up appointment
  for yourself and
  bridesmaids
Book spray tan appointment

TRANSPORT

Decide how many cars are
  required
Book transport for guests if
  required
Inform car company if
  second venue is required
  for photos
Choose colour ribbons
Send direction maps to
  guests if necessary

PHOTOGRAPHY

Choose photographer
Choose videographer if
  required
Discuss package(s) required
Discuss style of photography
  – formal/informal
Choose second venue if
  required
Make list of photos required

FLOWERS

Choose colour scheme
Choose shape and style of bouquets
Choose flowers for bouquets
Order buttonholes and corsages
Order flowers for the church (with other couples if appropriate)
Order thank you bouquets for mothers

HONEYMOON

Decide where to go
Book holiday and pay deposit
Change name on wife's passport
Vaccinations if necessary
Book transport to airport if required

THANK YOUS

Make present list as gifts arrive
Write thank you letters or cards
Send cake to guests unable to attend wedding

Index

"Now you will feel no rain,
for each of you will be shelter
for the other

Now you will feel no cold,
for each of you will be warmth
for the other

Now there is no more loneliness

Now you are two persons
but there is one life before you

May your days together be
good and long upon the earth."

Apache wedding blessing

'The Greatest Tips in the World' books

Pet Recipe books

The Greatest Feline Feasts in the World by Joe Inglis
ISBN 978-1-905151-50-9

The Greatest Doggie Dinners in the World by Joe Inglis
ISBN 978-1-905151-51-6

'The Greatest in the World' DVDs

The Greatest in the World – Gardening Tips
presented by Steve Brookes

The Greatest in the World – Yoga Tips
presented by David Gellineau and David Robson

The Greatest in the World – Cat & Kitten Tips
presented by Joe Inglis

The Greatest in the World – Dog & Puppy Tips
presented by Joe Inglis

For more information about currently available
and forthcoming book and DVD titles please visit:

www.thegreatestintheworld.com

The GREATEST in the WORLD

or write to:

The Greatest in the World Ltd
PO Box 3182
Stratford-upon-Avon
Warwickshire CV37 7XW
United Kingdom

Tel / Fax: +44(0)1789 299616
Email: info@thegreatestintheworld.com

The author

Jill and her husband Colin started their wedding car business in Plymouth in 1996 with gorgeous vintage ivory cars. The business was a great success and since then, she has 'been to' hundreds of weddings of all types, and in all sorts of venues.

Until then her main job had been teaching English, usually to adults, and she still runs some short courses and marks what seems like mountains of exam papers every year! In addition, she writes children's books and short stories for women's magazines.

In her spare time, she enjoys walking in the glorious Devon countryside.

Acknowledgements:

My thanks for help and advice go to:

Jennifer Baker Photography, Harewood Cars, Belair Video, Prudence Gowns, Marldon Marquees, Celebration Balloons, Amanda Dow (beautician), Kelly at Toni and Guy.